Enameling
Made Easy

Torch-Firing **Workshop**
for Beginners & Beyond

Enameling Made Easy

Torch-Firing **Workshop** for Beginners & Beyond

KB

KALMBACH BOOKS

Anat Silvera

*To all my students,
past, present,
and future*

Kalmbach Books
21027 Crossroads Circle
Waukesha, Wisconsin 53186
www.Kalmbach.com/Books

Please follow appropriate health and safety measures when working with materials and equipment. Some general guidelines are presented in this book, but always read and follow manufacturers' instructions.

Every effort has been made to ensure the accuracy of the information presented; however, the publisher is not responsible for any injuries, losses, or other damages that may result from the use of the information in this book.

Published in 2014
18 17 16 15 14   1 2 3 4 5

Manufactured in China

ISBN: 978-0-87116-770-5
EISBN: 978-1-62700-106-9

Editor: Mary Wohlgemuth
Art Director: Lisa Bergman
Photographers: James Forbes, William Zuback

Publisher's Cataloging-in-Publication Data
Silvera, Anat.
    Enameling made easy : torch-firing workshop for beginners & beyond / Anat Silvera.

        p. : col. ill. ; cm. + 1 DVD (sd., col. ; 4¾ in.)

    Includes index.
    Accompanying DVD includes demonstrations of: using a sifter; firing stages; embedding wire, seed beads, and threaders; wet-packing for cloisonné; and other enameling techniques.

    Issued also as an ebook.
    ISBN: 978-0-87116-770-5

    1. Enamel and enameling–Handbooks, manuals, etc. 2. Jewelry making–Handbooks, manuals, etc.
    3. Metal-work–Handbooks, manuals, etc. I. Title.

TT382.6 .S55 2014
739.275

Contents

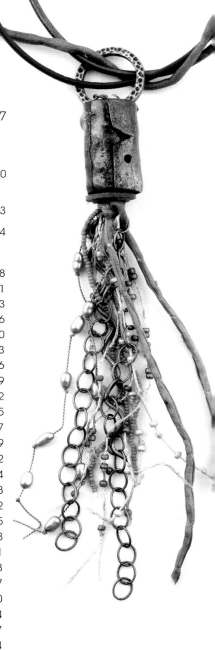

Introduction

Enameling is the art of fusing glass to metal, either in a kiln or with a torch. It is a complex and rich art form that comprises multiple techniques and methods. My goal with this book is to whet your appetite with an easy, affordable way to bring enamel into your work and your world.

You may have been curious and wanted to learn about enameling, but thought that your only option was using a kiln or a torch setup with big tanks. This book is for you. My approach is accessible because it uses a handheld butane torch. It is affordable due to the short list of necessary yet small tools and equipment. Working with a torch intimately involves you with the process, and the immediacy of the technique is addicting. Within a short time, you'll be creating beautiful enameled jewelry.

There are many methods for coloring metal, but there is a special sense of freedom and movement watching glass flow and fuse to metal. This book introduces you to the richness of this medium, showing you how magical and exciting it is with concrete projects that take you step by step through some basic techniques for creating jewelry. You'll discover multiple ways to create depth and texture with enamel as well as hone your metalsmithing skills. Endless possibilities will unfold as you begin to experience and appreciate the subtleties of working with enamel.

Practicing a craft such as enameling on a daily basis is like cultivating a garden. You get to delight in the process, your progress, and the lovely, colorful results.

About the book and DVD

This book-with-DVD is designed to give you all the benefits of a workshop—with all the convenience of learning how to enamel at home. The Getting Started section introduces the fundamentals of adding enamel color to metal. Lists of toolkits and supplies on p. 44–45 will help you pull together what you need to get started. The jewelry projects, beginning with the easiest and gradually getting more challenging, give you hands-on experience to build your confidence.

The video disk enclosed in the back of the book includes 12 short lessons. Icons throughout the book indicate that you can see a technique in close-up action on your screen as I explain it.

Getting Started

Enameling seems like magic to me. Colors combine, flow, and change as they go from powder to liquid, and then they slowly cool from red hot into beautiful color.

In this section you'll become acquainted with the terms, techniques, and tools you'll need to begin making your own enameling magic.

You'll also find a primer on metalworking techniques you'll use in conjunction with enameling, along with a handy guide to all the tools and supplies you'll need for the jewelry projects that follow.

ENAMELING BASICS

What is enameling?

Enameling is the art of fusing glass onto metal. Fine grains of transparent or opaque glass are applied to metal and fused with high heat in a kiln or from a torch flame. After fusing, the colors remain intact without fading. You may sometimes hear this technique referred to as *vitreous enameling*, which references the Latin word for glass, *vitrum*.

The art of enameling has been around for centuries, as seen in jewelry worldwide and ornamentation on ancient weaponry, religious objects, and vessels. The brilliant, jewel-like quality of enamel was often used instead of gemstones. Enameling became especially popular in the late 19th to early 20th century when it was used in Art Nouveau jewelry and became synonymous with craftsmen like René Lalique. The 21st century is an exciting period for the craft because of the resurgence of appreciation for and awareness of enameling, with more and more metalsmiths incorporating it into their work. So many resources exist today for learning about the craft: enamelist societies, classes, DVDs, websites, and, of course, books. We can be inspired by how artists all over the world explore the brilliant beauty of enamel.

What is torch-fired enameling?

When people think of enameling, they usually picture firing in a kiln, which is the traditional way of enameling jewelry and large objects. In the mid-20th century, pioneers including Fred Ball and Joseph Spencer experimented with methods for firing enamel by applying heat directly with a torch.

Working with a torch is affordable and intimate. The flame puts you right there with the process, since it isn't hidden inside the kiln, and you can control the application of heat in a way that can't be matched by a kiln. You get to see the magic firsthand when the glass transforms and fuses to the metal.

On the other hand, using a kiln allows the artist to fire large pieces and multiple pieces at the same time. The heat is more uniform, and with some techniques, you'll have more-consistent results. But with a little practice, a torch can not only create a wide variety of enamel finishes, but can also tackle techniques like cloisonné, champlevé, raku, and plique-à-jour.

This book focuses on torch-fired enameling and does not cover kiln techniques. Common torches that can be used for enameling include mini propane torches designed for weed control, larger propane or MAPP gas torches commonly used by plumbers, a two-gas (oxygen and acetylene) setup, and butane. Each fuel type influences the color of the enamel.

Of these, handheld butane torches are the most accessible and affordable, and they do not require as much room or as many safety measures as do tank torches. You'll be able to enamel all the projects in this book using a butane torch; most projects use the large-flame type shown here.

Large-flame butane torch.

All the projects in this book use a handheld butane torch for firing enamel.

Enameling techniques

Simple application of enamel to metal can create beautiful results, and many of the projects use that fundamental skill. Here's an introduction to specialty techniques that go beyond the basics and can be created with torch-firing. If a project in the book uses a technique, I've referenced the project page that will tell you more about it. Some techniques are demonstrated on the DVD as well.

Cloisonné

Perhaps the most well known of enamel techniques, cloisonné begins with creating small cells with wire on an enameled surface. Those cells are filled and fired with multiple layers of enamel. Cloisonné can be left partially filled, or sanded with abrasive stones so the enamels and wires are flush at the surface. **Cloisonné Lines Pendant, p. 103; Cityscape Pendant, p. 107.**

Plique-à-jour

Similar to the look of cloisonné, the plique-à-jour technique suspends enamel in cells that have no backing, allowing light to shine through like stained glass. **Plique-à-Jour Dots Earrings, p. 111.**

Sgraffito

In sgraffito, you create patterns by drawing through a layer of sifted, dry enamel to reveal previous layers of enamel or the metal base. Simple tools like scribes and brushes can be used to shift and shape the enamel powder. **Sgraffito Tab-Set Pendant, p. 84.**

Stenciling

Sifting enamels through a pierced material allows you to transfer a pattern that is then fired. Stencils can be custom-made, purchased, or made from found objects such metal screens, mesh, and lace. **Stenciled Pendant, p. 56.**

Raku

Borrowed from the ceramics world, this technique creates unpredictable changes in the enamel colors and surface. While the piece is still red-hot, it is placed in a combustible material like newspaper and sealed inside a container. The sudden reduction in oxygen creates interesting effects.

Stamping

A rubber stamp is used with archival ink to stamp a design, and then enamel is sifted over it. When the piece is overturned, enamel powder adheres only to the stamped design, and the enamel is fired. **Stamped Dog Tag, p. 60.**

Basse-taille

In basse-taille, textured metal is covered with transparent enamels. The lovely surface of the metal below glows through the layers of glass.

Champlevé

To create champlevé, deeply recessed areas in metal are created by etching, engraving, or fabrication, and are then filled with wet enamel. After firing layers of enamel to fill these depressions, the raised metal is polished.

Painting

Watercolor, acrylic paints, and even crayons can be incorporated into enameled surfaces.

Workspace safety

As long as you follow simple, commonsense rules, torch-fired enameling is safe to do at home or in your studio. Using enamels that don't contain lead and practicing torch and materials safety are the most important safety measures.

Enamels come in lead-bearing and lead-free colors. I recommend that you use only lead-free enamels to avoid any exposure to lead or to toxic fumes as leaded enamel is fired.

Work in a space with windows or doors that can be opened to circulate air. Don't set up in a small enclosed space, like a walk-in closet.

Any kind of enamel powder can irritate your eyes, lungs, and throat, so wear didymium or clear safety glasses as you clean and sift the enamel and a lightweight respirator or a dust mask rated for glass particulates or sanding. Avoid drafts, which can blow the enamels around.

An exhaust fan directly above your work area is excellent for drawing away airborne particles or fumes, but if this isn't possible, use a tabletop exhaust fan with a filter or an air purifier.

This is not a craft to do on your kitchen table. Do not eat or drink in your enameling area and damp-wipe all the surfaces often—especially when you are done for the day. Wash your hands after enameling, damp-mop or vacuum the floor, and clean your work clothes.

Protect your eyes as you torch-fire by wearing safety glasses with UV and IR protection, like calobar or didymium lenses. Glare from the glass on metal can cause cataracts and retinal problems over time.

Never keep fuel on your work table or near an open flame; store it away from the torch. Keep a fire extinguisher in your work area. Protect yourself with an apron made of natural fiber in case anything hot falls on you (synthetics melt!). Tie back loose hair, and keep jewelry and clothing away from the flame.

Use a respirator (above) or a good-quality dust mask as you clean and sift enamels. Use safety glasses with UV and IR protection (left) while firing.

How to fill a butane torch

To ensure good results with a butane torch and to maintain it for a long life, use high-quality butane. Purchase butane canisters at hardware stores and specialty stores that cater to jewelry-making, cooking, or smokers. Choose a fuel canister with a nozzle that matches the fuel port on your torch.

Wear safety glasses and always fuel your torch in a well-ventilated place away from open flames. If fueling outdoors, be aware of the wind direction and avoid fuel blowing in your direction.

Make sure the flame is extinguished and any safety switches are in lock mode. Remove the stand and locate the brass fuel port on the bottom of the torch **[A]**.

Shake the butane canister gently to warm it up. With the torch upside down in one hand and the butane in the other, extend your arms, place the nozzle on the butane canister into the port, and press down hard to make a tight seal **[B]**. As you fill the torch, you'll hear a slight hissing and see haze.

A backspray of wet butane tells you the torch is full. Stop fueling immediately. Overfilling may cause fuel to spit out of the fuel port or flame nozzle. Don't use the torch until any spitting has stopped.

Place the torch upright in its stand. Let it sit for 10–15 minutes to allow any air bubbles to settle. Air bubbles can cause the flame to sputter, extinguish, or flare erratically. When the air bubble clears, the torch will return to normal function.

Lighting a large-flame torch

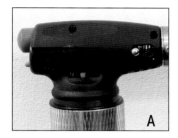  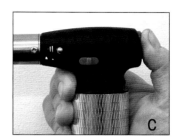

First, some general safety advice: Never let go of a torch if it is lit; turn it off first for safety. Read and follow the instructions that came with your torch.

To light, turn the gas lever to slightly less than the midpoint between the minus (–) and plus (+) marks. This avoids igniting the flame on maximum **[A]**.

Depress the red safety switch under the large red trigger button. You should hear a click **[B]**.

Point the torch toward a firesafe surface such as a kiln brick (also known as a firebrick). Push the trigger down firmly to ignite the torch. If it doesn't light, release the safety switch and repeat the process until it ignites **[C]**.

After the torch lights, with the trigger still depressed, slide the locking switch on the left side of the torch toward the trigger and release the trigger. This will keep the flame going without stressing your thumb **[D]**.

To turn off the torch, slide the locking switch toward the flame nozzle. Check to make sure the flame is out **[E]**.

Store the butane torch upright. The nozzle stays hot for a while after use, so don't lay it down; place the torch in its stand.

Lighting a Blazer torch

Open the gas knob to start the flow of butane **[A]**.

Point the torch toward a firesafe surface such as a kiln brick. Depress the trigger completely to light the flame **[B]**. Repeat until the flame ignites. When you release the trigger, the flame will stay on.

To turn off the torch, close the gas knob completely to turn off the fuel, which will extinguish the flame.

Torch troubleshooting

If the torch fails to ignite and you smell butane, stop and wait until the butane clears before continuing.

Sometimes ignitors may fail over time, but the torch may still operate. Use another method to ignite the flame, like a torch lighter (sparker). Cup the butane with the torch lighter and squeeze the handle to spark the flint and ignite the butane.

The torch may not light because it doesn't have enough fuel. Try increasing the amount of gas with the gas lever or fuel knob. Depress the trigger or turn on the fuel knob and listen for the hiss of butane. No hiss? No fuel!

If you suspect the torch is broken or malfunctioning, don't use it.

Setting up your work areas

The surface of your enameling prep area should be easy to clean after sifting. Use a baking pan with a shallow lip. Store enamel colors in separate labeled containers, and keep the containers closed when not in use. Keep a stack of glossy magazine pages handy so you can use a clean sheet as you sift each enamel color. Pour uncontaminated enamel back into its container. Fold the glossy paper in half, then in half again, and dispose of it.

Create a firesafe area for torch-firing enamel. Use a 12" (31cm) square ceramic floor tile as a fireproof surface to protect your table. Use several K23 soft kiln bricks from a ceramic supplier to support and raise enameling trivets. I keep one brick on a 4" (10cm) square plastic turntable so I can access the trivet from all angles.

Projects with holes are best torch-fired from underneath. Use a tripod with a steel mesh screen to raise the piece for firing.

Keep your torch area clear of flammable materials, like paper and fabric, and keep butane canisters away from the torch-firing station. Point the flame only toward firesafe surfaces, like the kiln brick.

Keep enameling supplies and your torch-firing station separate from any soldering tools and your soldering station (see p. 33).

Create one station for enameling prep work and another for torch-firing.

Choosing metals for enameling

Enamel adheres best to metals that don't contain zinc and have a high enough melting point to withstand enameling temperatures above 1200°F (649°C). Fine silver, copper, gold (18kt or higher), and steel work well. My favorite metal to enamel is copper. Copper is inexpensive and versatile. You can cover it up with an opaque color, expose it with sgraffito, or highlight textured copper with transparent colors.

Traditionally, when using gold or silver, enamelists avoid opaque colors because they hide the beauty of the metal. Also, silver and gold can change and enhance the colors fired over them. An inexpensive way to allow gold or silver color to show through transparent enamel is to add gold or silver foil to enamel-coated copper.

Zinc keeps enamels from adhering well to metal, and many common alloys like brass contain zinc. Enamel applied to these metals may crack or simply not bond. Other metals such as sterling silver, Argentium sterling silver, and low karats of gold that have relatively low melting points can melt during enameling.

TIP

Some copper comes with a plastic coating on one side. Remove it before firing.

Metals for torch-fired enameling		
Preferred	**Difficult**	**Not recommended**
Fine silver	Sterling silver	14kt gold or lower
Copper	Argentium sterling	Nickel
18kt gold or higher	Brass	Zinc
Steel		Low-melting-point metals such as tin

enameling on brass

If you choose to experiment with enameling on brass or unknown alloys, clean the metal thoroughly to help the enamel adhere. Rinse and dry. Keep a shallow ceramic dish handy to cover the piece if you hear any pinging (which indicates cracking); quickly cover the piece while it's still on the trivet to keep any flying glass contained, and let it cool. These lovely enameled flowers started as brass findings I bought at a local bead store.

Size and gauge

The size and temperature of the flame determines the size and gauge of metal that can be enameled. With the torches used in this book, use 18–24-gauge metal that is no larger than 2" (51mm) square. If a piece is too big, the enamel won't reach fusing temperature. If a piece is too thick, you won't be able to fire on as many coats of enamel, and the piece will be heavy. If the metal is too thin, it may warp.

Choosing enamels

Purchasing enamels can be overwhelming because there are so many kinds: different mesh sizes, which tells you how fine the grains are; soft, medium, and hard fusing temperatures; transparent, opaque, and opalescent; powders, paints, and more. I'll make it simple for you: All my projects use lead-free, medium-temperature, medium-expansion, 80-mesh enamels, which are recommended for use on silver, copper, or gold. All that's left is for you to choose your colors.

Enamel colors are usually identified with a number or code. Thompson Enamel, the U.S. manufacturer of the enamels used in this book, identifies opaque colors with 1000-series numbers and transparent colors with 2000-series numbers. Thompson sells sample kits of the entire range of colors, and resellers offer small amounts of individual colors too. If your enamel powders arrive in plastic bags, I recommend carefully transferring them to plastic containers; plastic bags can get punctured and you could lose a lot of enamel, and it's much easier to scoop powder out of a container. (Wear a mask as you transfer the powder.) Remember to label all your containers.

Fired enamel can look completely different than the powdered color or a seller's printed sample. Color will vary depending on the kind of gas used, level of firing, and other variables. (See "Making color samples," p. 28.)

Dry enamel powders can last a long time if they are kept cool and dry. Don't allow contaminants or other colors to mix in the containers. Any enamels contaminated by accidentally mixing colors can be used as *counterenamel* (see p. 22).

Cleaning enamels

Most of the projects in this book use dry, sifted enamels. Washing the enamel removes fines, which are fine particles of enamel that can cause cloudiness or distort colors. Transparent colors are better if washed first, and some techniques like cloisonné require enamels to be washed. After washing, they can be dried and sifted as usual. Unless used for cloisonné, washing opaque colors is optional. Enamels must be completely dry before firing or they can pop off.

Use distilled water, since tap water has impurities. Wash only what you need, because wet enamels go farther and don't last as long as powdered enamels. In fact, humidity and temperature can affect the quality of most enamels. Store all enamels, washed or dry, in a tightly covered jar in a dry area away from the sun, and label each jar with the color name and number.

To wash your enamels, place the enamel in a glass jar or plastic container with a lid. Add about 2–3 times more water than enamel. Tighten the lid, and swirl the water and enamel together.

Let the enamel settle to the bottom. Pour the cloudy water directly into a second container or through a coffee filter. You can recover the fines that remain in the filter and use those for counterenamel. The lip on a baby food jar keeps the enamel back, allowing just the water to pour out. Repeat the washing process until the water is completely clear after the enamel settles.

FAQ

How can I dry the enamel before firing? When I've used a kiln for enameling, I placed the piece on a trivet on top of the hot kiln to help it dry faster.
Place the piece on a trivet on a kiln brick and gently heat the brick for 15 seconds to a bright red. The heat from the brick will help dry the enamel faster. Wait until the enamel is dry before firing.

Cleaning metal

For enamels to fuse, metal must be clean and free of oils and *firescale* (discoloration caused by oxygen and the torch flame reacting with copper). If you want to punch holes, do it before cleaning and enameling. Always clean the metal before enameling.

Citric acid pickle, heated in a crock pot until it steams, is a great solution for cleaning metal. Soak the metal for at least 3 minutes, rinse, and dry. Scrubbing with Penny Brite, a cleaner designed for copper cookware, is a good alternative to pickling.

After firing, the counterenamel side of the piece (the side nearest the flame) will have firescale. (See p. 22 for more information on counterenameling.) To clean it takes a bit of work. A 10-minute soak in the pickle solution will remove most of the discoloration. To use the copper cleaner to remove firescale, use a hard toothbrush, a green scouring pad, or even your fingertip to scrub thoroughly, and rinse well.

If pickling or Penny Brite doesn't remove all of the firescale, use 320-grit wet/dry sandpaper.

Scrubbing the piece with Penny Brite often removes firescale quickly.

Counterenameling

The stress of expansion and contraction when metal is heated can be lessened by evenly sifting and fusing enamel on the back of a piece first. This is called *counterenameling*. By counterenameling the back and then putting a base coat on the front, you create a stable enameled piece and protect it from cracking and warping.

Counterenamel can be a single color, a mix of colors left over after sifting, or one of Thompson Enamel's clear colors such as 2030, a great all-purpose clear enamel that the manufacturer calls "medium fusing clear." Using mixed counterenamel produces a confetti-like look. If you use the same color as on the front, be aware that the heat applied to fuse the enamel to the front will create dark spots on the back, giving it a different appearance.

Dapping strengthens metal, so a domed piece is not likely to warp (unlike a flat piece). It's not necessary to counterenamel a domed piece, but I often do it anyway for aesthetic reasons.

FAQ Is one coat of counterenamel enough to prevent warping and
cracking if I want to add multiple coats on the front of my piece? One even coat of counterenamel is enough for several coats on the front. If you want more than three top coats or if the counterenamel layer is thin, fire two coats of counterenamel.

Your first enameling step in most projects is applying and firing a base coat on the back, called counterenameling. A mix of colors produces a speckled effect when fired.

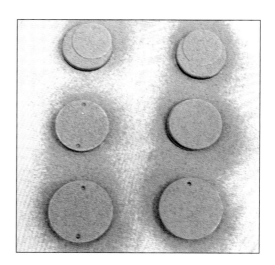

Sifting enamel

Sifting is how you add enamel powder to the metal or enamel base using screens of various sizes and meshes. For the projects in this book, we will use only small, medium, and line-size sifters with 80-mesh screens. Using finer screens on subsequent coats can smooth out layers, add rich color, and fill in for more coverage.

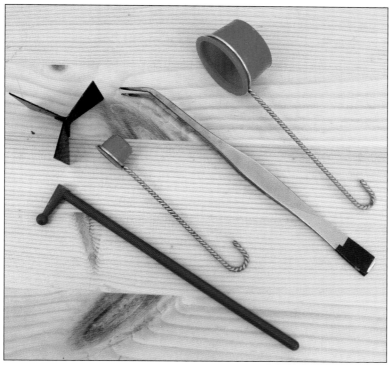

Sifting supplies (clockwise from upper right): Medium sifter, tweezers, small sifter, line sifter, and trivet.

Basics of sifting

First rule: Make any holes in metal before you sift or fire the enamel.

I create little pedestals for sifting by stacking two pennies—it will be easy to pick up the metal later. (Use epoxy to glue the pennies together to keep the pedestals steady and make cleaning easy.) Place the pedestals on a clean sheet of slick magazine paper. Place the clean metal ready for sifting on the pedestals.

The distance from which you sift affects the enamel application. Sift 2–3" (51–76mm) above the piece to create a thin, even coat. Sift in a circular motion, from the inside out. Don't worry if the first coat is not even or level. You can always sift on another coat after firing to even it out. You can even apply a third coat to create a slightly domed effect.

Three ways to sift

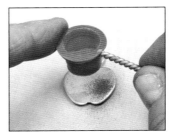

1. Fill the sifter one-third full. Hold it in your dominant hand, cupping the end in your palm with the pinky finger and the finger next to it. Place your thumb on the neck. With your index finger, rub the wire ridges to release the enamel.

2. Hold the sifter the same as in #1, but this time use your index finger to gently tap the sifter to release the enamel.

3. This method uses both hands. Hold the sifter as before, but use the index finger of your other hand to gently tap the side of the sifter and release the enamel.

TIP
To prevent contamination of your enamels, clean the sifter with a dry brush after sifting each color and tap off any enamel left on the pennies. (A wet brush could cause the sifter to rust.)

Transferring the piece to the trivet
Practice transferring before you sift on any enamel. To transfer a sifted piece to the trivet, grasp the sides of the piece with tweezers or use a palette knife under the piece. If the piece has a drilled hole, place the tips of the tweezers in the hole and lift straight up, keeping it level as you place it in the trivet. Grabbing the sides of the piece to move it to the trivet takes some practice to avoid disturbing the enamel. You can set up the pedestals so the piece rests on the edge of each one with a space between; after sifting, you can easily pick up the piece with a palette knife.

FAQ

I accidentally filled the punched holes with enamel when I sifted. What can I do?
Catch it right away before you fire. Keep an awl handy to place in the hole to release
the enamel. Another way is to set the piece down with one hole at 12 o'clock so you
remember the location. When you place the tweezers in the hole to pick it up to move
it to the trivet, the enamel should fall out of the hole. Also, tapping the piece gently
against the kiln brick without disturbing the rest of the enamel can clear the hole. If
you make a mistake and fired enamel fills the hole, you can always use the piece as
a cabochon.

Can I mix enamels to make a new color?
No. Enamel powders don't blend like paint. (Watercolor enamels, not used in this
book, can be mixed to make new colors.) The grains will fire separately, with a confetti
effect, which is one of my favorite tricks for making a speckled counterenamel. You
can modify colors with layers of transparent enamels, using them like glazes. It is fun
to experiment with an opaque color as a base coat and a transparent color fired on
top. The results are lovely new colors.

**If I have a piece that is not flat, like a dome or angled shape, how do I keep the
enamel from sliding off or clumping?**
Spray the piece with a holding agent, like nonaerosol hairspray or a 50/50 solution
of Klyr-Fire and distilled water in a Preval sprayer, which converts the liquid into an
atomized mist. Sift and allow to dry before firing. The holding agent keeps the enamel
grains in place. If you have a bead cap with a hole, place a skewer through the hole
and hold it upright while you sift.

Why can't I place the piece on a trivet on the kiln brick and sift directly onto it?
You will get enamels on the trivet. When fired, the enamel will melt and fuse your
piece and the trivet together. They will be almost impossible to separate without
ruining your piece, and the trivet will be contaminated. Sifting directly over the kiln
brick also wastes enamel, because you can't collect the leftovers, which fall into the
crevices of the brick or mix with the dust. There are a few exceptions: Sometimes
details can be applied with a line sifter while the piece is on the trivet.

**If I sifted too much enamel on one section of my piece and I want it to be more
even, do I have to tap off the enamel and start over?**
No! Gently tap the enamel with the screen of the sifter to even out the coat. If it
doesn't work, remove the enamel and sift again.

Torch-firing on a trivet

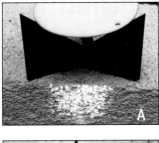  

 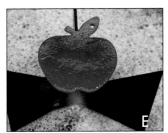 

Place the trivet near the edge of a kiln brick. Turn on the torch and adjust the gas lever on the side of the torch to create a medium-size flame. Avoid shocking the enamel by first aiming the flame at the edge of kiln brick, just below the trivet **[A]**. (This is especially important as you progress to using any holding agents, embedded glass, or metal. If you're too fast with the heat, enamel and parts can start popping off.)

Move the flame to the trivet, heating the steel below your piece **[B]**.

As soon as the enamel begins to change color, aim the flame directly under the piece on the trivet **[C]**.

 The first stage of firing is sugar coat, which looks like a dark sandy surface **[D]**. The second stage is called orange peel, because the bright red enamel surface looks dimpled **[E]**.

The final stage is called glossy. When the enamel is fully fused, it appears slick and smooth with an orange glow **[F]**. Sometimes it helps to look at the surface from an angle to see if all the bumps have disappeared.

TIP

When firing pieces with large holes, like washers and donut shapes, place the trivet on a mesh screen on top of a tripod. Because the steel mesh screen is a heat sink that can slow down the firing, cut a small hole in it and place the trivet on top. This lets you evenly heat the back of the piece through the trivet, which helps prevent darkened spots on the front.

When the surface is smooth and glossy, remove the heat and turn off the torch. Let the enamel cool for at least one minute; it will start to turn its final color **[G]**. Remove the piece from the trivet with tweezers and let the piece cool on the tile or kiln brick. Don't be discouraged by dark hues when done firing. Wait for the magic as the enamel fully cools and the true color is revealed.

FAQ

What if my piece sticks to the trivet after firing?
Pick up the hot trivet carefully with your tweezers and tap the base of the trivet against the tile. If the piece doesn't release, flip it over and tap the top of the trivet against the tile. Usually one of these two taps will do it!

Why can't I just fire my enamels from above instead of from underneath?
Firing directly over enamels can change the color, especially opaques, which get dark and muddy. Truer colors are achieved by firing from below. However, sometimes it's possible to fire transparent colors from above, as I demonstrate in the Soldered Reversible Pendant project, p. 114.

Overfired piece.

What does it look like if I overfire a piece?
Overfiring can cause pits and will darken the color.

If I am unhappy with the results after firing a piece, do I just throw it away?
No! More often than not, a piece can be reworked into something better. Sift and fire an opaque color over the entire piece to make a blank canvas for starting over. You can also get creative: Sift more colors or add patterns of enamels with a stencil or stamps. You might be surprised by how much you learn from and love your mistake. It's one of my favorite qualities about enameling!

Underfired piece. The enamel has an orange-peel appearance.

What if I've used two layers of enamel and I don't like how it turned out? Is it too much to add more enamel?
Yes, adding more layers could be too heavy and warp your piece. If it's a flat piece, flip it over and use the old front as your new counterenamel side. As long as you used only one layer of counterenamel, adding another layer to this new front will be fine.

If I don't like the shiny enamel and I want a matte finish, what can I do?
The quickest and most reliable way is to use a glass etchant, available at craft stores.

Making color samples

Powdered enamels can look very different from their fired colors. And although most shops or websites display a sample firing of each color, your results will vary because of the gas used, firing time, and other variables. Making a sample of each color is good practice and gives you a great reference for designing.

I recommend two simple methods for making samples. The first is to fire samples of each color on uniform size and gauge disks. (I used pre-1980 U.S. pennies, which work best because of the copper content.) Punch a hole in each disk, clean, and counterenamel. For the opaques, fire two coats on the front of each one. For the transparent colors, fire on a layer of undercoat white and then fire one coat of the transparent color. Label each sample with the color name and number.

Another experiment you can try will give you a range of effects for transparent colors. Cut a 1x2" (26x51mm) piece of 22-gauge copper sheet, clean it, and counterenamel it. Divide the front into four equal ½" (13mm) sections. Use one section for a layer of undercoat white, on another fire just a coat of 2030 Medium Fusing

TRANSPARENT COLORS (Thompson Enamels)

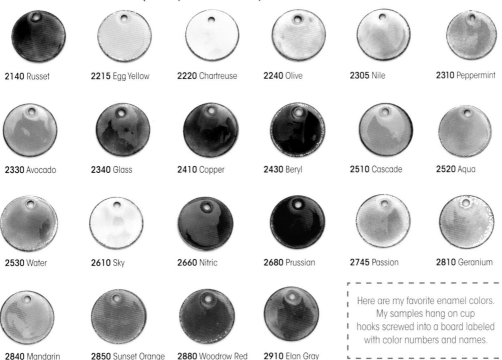

2140 Russet	2215 Egg Yellow	2220 Chartreuse	2240 Olive	2305 Nile	2310 Peppermint
2330 Avocado	2340 Glass	2410 Copper	2430 Beryl	2510 Cascade	2520 Aqua
2530 Water	2610 Sky	2660 Nitric	2680 Prussian	2745 Passion	2810 Geranium
2840 Mandarin	2850 Sunset Orange	2880 Woodrow Red	2910 Elan Gray		

Here are my favorite enamel colors. My samples hang on cup hooks screwed into a board labeled with color numbers and names.

Clear, and on the third, fire the transparent directly onto the copper. On the last section, use a piece of silver foil: Fire on some clear enamel, add the foil, and then add another layer of clear. Finally, fire a coat of the transparent color over the entire piece. Notice how different the colors look over different bases!

OPAQUE COLORS

1010 Undercoat   1125 Nut

1150 Woodrow   1170 Elk   1202 Off White   1208 Cream   1224 Melon   1240 Pine

1308 Lichen   1315 Willow   1319 Bitter   1335 Pea   1360 Jungle   1410 Robin's Egg

1415 Seafoam   1425 Sapphire   1430 Spruce   1465 Peacock   1510 Ozone   1520 Calamine

1560 Bluejay   1660 Ultramarine   1685 Cobalt   1705 Petal   1715 Clover   1760 Iris

1780 Grape   1810 Buttercup   1830 Marigold   1850 Pumpkin   1860 Flame Orange   1870 Orient

1880 Flame Red   1890 Victoria   1915 Dove   1920 Stump   1940 Steel   1995 Black

Troubleshooting

When learning any new craft, it's common and easy to make mistakes. Don't stress! Fixing those mistakes is part of learning and mastering enameling. Here are some common mistakes and my suggestions for fixing them or avoiding them next time.

The enamel chips off or falls off.	
Why?	**How to fix it**
The metal was not hot enough and the enamel did not adhere properly	Simply flash-fire, which is to refire the piece and take it to the glossy stage.
The metal was not compatible with the enamel (see "Choosing enamels" and "Choosing metals for enameling")	Use the recommended metals.
The metal was dirty and prevented the enamel from fusing	Clean the metal more thoroughly next time: Remove any firescale. Clean the metal. Remove any residue from cleaning. Sift on more enamel and fire.
Quenching the enamel caused it to crack, crackle, or chip	Sand the cracked area with 320-grit wet/dry sandpaper, add a light coat of the same enamel color, refire, and allow it to cool without quenching.
Not counterenameling a flat piece of metal created tension that caused the enamel to crack or warp	Always counterenamel the back first. To fix this piece, counterenamel the back, which will change the color on the front during firing. Sift more enamel on the front and refire. Alternatively, use the existing front as the back (counterenamel side). Clean the counterenamel side and prepare it for enameling. Sift and fire with enamel to make this the new front. If your piece warps while the enamel is still warm, immediately transfer it to a heat-safe surface and cover it with a heavy weight such as an old steel block.

The enamel has lots of bubbles, pits, or holes, or it pulls away after firing.	
Why?	**How to fix it**
The enamel was still wet when fired	Use a line sifter or small straw to fill in the holes. Or sift over the entire piece, allowing it to dry thoroughly, and refire.
The coat of enamel was either too thin or too thick	There isn't much you can do if the coat of enamel was too thick, except try to work with the results. If it was too thin, add another layer and refire.
Small bubbles formed	It's likely that the enamel was underfired. Just fire again until the surface is glossy.
Pits and bubbles appeared	Overfiring may be the culprit. Fill in holes with fresh enamel and refire. It's helpful to rough up the surface with 320-grit sandpaper to help the enamel stay in place during firing.
The enamel pulls away like a wave	This usually means the metal wasn't clean; clean it more thoroughly next time. This situation is hard to fix. Clean the exposed metal and sand the enamel with 320-grit sandpaper. Refire; the enamel may settle down.
The enamel surface has holes	The enamel may have been contaminated. Fill in holes with new enamel and refire. Make sure the enamel you return to the jar contains no dirt, firescale, or bits of kiln brick.

There are endless ways to add interest to your surfaces with enameling. I encourage you to try different experiments and write down what you do so you can try it again.

Here are a few of my favorite special-effects ideas.

Special effects

Metal filings
Sprinkling metal filings into your enamels adds a rough or smooth speckled pattern. Capture filing dust in a tray below where you work with metal. Keep the dust in separate, labeled containers. Sprinkle copper, silver, or gold dust onto a fired enamel surface, and fire to a glossy coat. The surface may be rough, which is a great effect. To create a smooth surface, fire a coat of 2030 clear over it. The effect varies with the colors fired.

Graphite
Graphite pencil lines resist enamel during firing, separating colors and making a clear pattern of pitted lines. Draw lines with a #2 pencil on clean copper, sift, and fire. (If you want to draw onto enamel, first roughen the surface with sandpaper or an alundum stone so the graphite can adhere.) This is my ode to modern art!

Bubble
This playful texture of bubbles and bumps is created by breaking the rules and firing enamel over a wet holding agent. Spray clean copper with the holding agent, sift, and quickly scribe a few lines. Fire before it's dry, and watch the enamel bubble!

Raku
This technique transforms transparent enamels into shimmering, metallic colors. After firing, the piece is dropped into a metal pan full of combustible material, like shredded newspaper or dry leaves. The paper is quickly lit on fire with a butane torch and a cover placed over it, sealing it. The fire reduces oxygen inside the container, creating the raku effect.

DVD 12

Faux etch
This looks like an etched piece of copper, but it is actually a design stamped directly on firescale and then sifted with a transparent color and fired.

METALWORK BASICS

Soldering

Soldering is joining metal using high heat and an alloy called solder that melts at a lower temperature than the metal to be joined. Because enamel fuses to metal around the same temperature as most solder, solder with a high-temperature melting point must be used to make joins that can withstand enameling. *Eutectic silver solder* is the best type of jewelry solder to use with enameling.

You may already be familiar with silver jewelry solder, a mix of sterling silver and zinc, which can be used to solder sterling silver, fine silver, copper, brass, and nickel. This is not the same solder that is sold in hardware stores for plumbing or for stained glass (those are solders with relatively low melting points). Solder for jewelry making is available from jewelry suppliers.

Most soldering tasks combine the same eight steps in roughly the same order:

1. Keep it clean. Dirt, skin oil, tarnish, and grease can stop solder cold and push away flux, which you apply to help protect metal from firescale. Handle metal with tweezers as much as possible. Clean your piece with soapy water or by pickling it. Rinse it thoroughly before soldering. Solder in a separate area from your enameling and don't share tools such as mesh screens or tweezers: Leftover enamels can fuse to a tool during soldering and contaminate it. Similarly, dust and flux from soldering can mess up your enamels.

2. Close the join. The join should be as tight as possible. Solder is very good at flowing along a flush seam. It isn't good at filling gaps. Check your piece carefully for any gaps and fix them before soldering.

Keep your soldering setup separate from your torch-firing station. Practice the eight steps listed and you'll have a better understanding of how soldering works and what to fix when it doesn't.

3. Use flux. Flux helps solder to flow, minimizes firescale, helps you measure the temperature of the metal, helps solder stick in place and pieces to stay in position, and changes color when it starts to break down. Flux all pieces to be joined completely. Any surface left unfluxed will form firescale, which will stop solder from joining the metal.

4. Cut and flux the solder. A little bit of solder goes a long way! Use the minimum amount to fill the join without too much extra to have to polish off later. Flux the solder lightly to keep it clean, and to make it easier to pick up and stick in place.

5. Apply the solder. Solder wants to stick to warm flux and warm metal. Keep the metal warm but not too hot while you apply solder with tweezers or a pick. The flux should be clear, and the metal should be matte and clean-looking. It should not glow pink or red at all. If the metal is too hot, the solder will flow as soon as you touch it!

6. Heat evenly. Bring the torch close and move slowly over the metal to increase the heat for soldering. Evenly heat the entire piece, not just the join. Heat the rest of the metal first and then bring the heat to the join. Easy, medium, and hard solder will flow when the metal is a light to medium red. When the metal turns bright red, high-temperature eutectic solder will flow.

7. Move it before it sticks. Move the metal before it cools and sticks to the block or board. If it sticks, it's being held by hardened flux. Use a little heat from the torch to loosen the flux, and use your pick or tweezers to move it. Or quench it on the block with a little water to break the flux. Don't pry it up or you'll take chunks of charcoal or solder board with it.

8. Quench. Pickle. Rinse. Quench your metal in water before pickling. Pickle for 2–5 minutes for a quick cleaning before continuing to solder. Pickle for a longer time, 20 minutes or more, when all soldering is complete to remove as much firescale as possible. Rinse off the pickle solution in water. Pickle solution left on metal can discolor tools and interfere with soldering.

Avoid heat sinks while soldering. Materials that take heat away from the metal, like steel tweezers or a cold solder board, can prevent the metal from ever reaching soldering temperature. Holding with tweezers too close to the join can suck heat away from the metal. Hold the piece as far from the join with as little steel as possible. Similarly, soldering a medium-to-large piece on a cold solder board can make it hard to heat the metal. Working on surfaces such as charcoal, kiln brick, or honeycomb makes it easier to heat metal fast and efficiently.

Using a metal punch

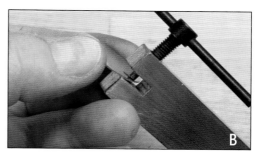

My hand punch for metal, which works with a screw-down action, has two punch sizes: The smaller punch makes a ¹⁄₁₆" (1.6mm) hole and the larger one makes a ³⁄₃₂" (2.4mm) hole. If the punch doesn't reach where you need a hole, use a drill (see "Drilling," p. 36).

Mark the spot where you want the hole to be with an indelible marker **[A]**.

Look at the piece from the side and place the punch on the mark **[B]**. Twist the handle clockwise until you feel it loosen. Reverse it until the punch exits the hole.

Another method may help you hit the mark better: Mark the spot and position the metal so you see the mark through the hole in the bottom of the punch **[C]**. Turn the handle to punch the hole. Sand the metal to remove any burrs.

To make holes at the bottom for dangling beads, draw a peace sign to indicate hole placement, and punch holes near the bottom **[D]**.

In effect, this screw-down punch is a small disk cutter, so it punches out a dot of metal for every hole. Save the dots—fine silver, sterling silver, gold, copper, and brass can be embedded in enamel for interesting color and texture.

Drilling

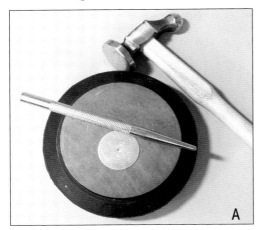

A

B

C

If a hand punch won't reach or you need a different size hole, you can use a flex shaft, a rotary tool, or a drill press to drill holes in your metal. Stationary drill presses are easy to use because the drill goes up and down evenly with a handle, and that's what I explain here. (Using a flex shaft or rotary tool is similar.) Use safety glasses, drill bits that are rated for metal, and read and follow the directions that came with your power tool.

To drill a hole, first use a center punch to create an indentation where you want to drill. Place the metal on a steel block, and use a chasing or ball-peen hammer to strike the punch **[A]**.

Drilling creates a lot of heat. Holding it with a ring clamp will prevent burns and injuries from spinning metal. Grasp the metal in a ring clamp, and tap the wedge until it's tight **[B]**. Place the metal on a flat, thick piece of scrap wood. With the drill off, practice placing the bit on the center punch mark **[C]**. Turn the motor to medium-high speed. Bring the handle down slowly to the mark and drill through gently, allowing the drill to do the cutting. Raise the handle to remove the bit from the hole and turn off the machine.

To make holes larger than ⅟₁₆", first drill a smaller hole, called a pilot hole. Use consecutively larger drill bits to expand the hole until you reach the final size. Using too large of a drill bit too quickly can jam in the metal and cause injuries.

Dapping

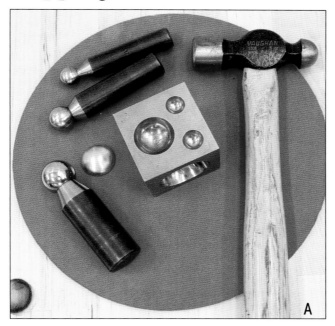

Use dapping sets to dome your metal. Dapping blocks and punches come in wood and metal (usually steel), and you strike the punches with an unpolished 8-oz. hammer **[A]** or brass mallet.

Find a depression that's a little larger than your disk. (Starting with a depression that's too close to the size of the disk will wrinkle the edges.) Find a dapping punch that's a little smaller than the depression. There should be enough room for the thickness of the metal disk **[B]**. Using too large a punch will damage the punch.

To dap, place the disk level inside the depression. Center the punch on the disk. Hit the punch with a hammer or mallet. Just a few hits should form the dome.

If you want a deeper dome, find the next size dap that fits your disk and a matching punch, and dap until the dome is the desired shape.

To remove any flat spots or wrinkles, angle the disk or the punch in the dap and strike the punch.

If a dome gets stuck in the block, turn it upside down and tap it with a hammer. The vibration can shake it loose.

Using the jeweler's saw

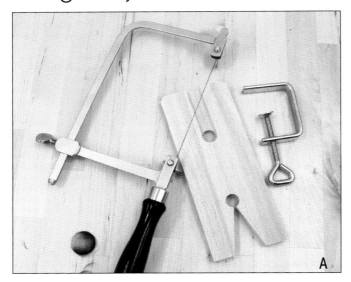

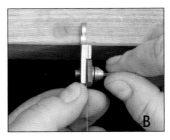

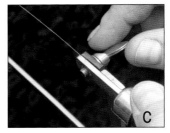

To saw metal, use a jeweler's saw frame with a V-slot bench pin and clamp **[A]**. The saw blade must be taut. A taut blade flexes very little when plucked.

Loading the saw

The teeth on the saw blade slant down toward the handle. They should feel smooth if stroked down toward the handle, and rough away. The teeth should face forward, away from the back of the frame. Clamp the top of the blade into the top clamp. The bottom of the blade should point straight toward the bottom clamp. Close the top clamp as tightly as you can by hand **[B]**.

Adjust the frame to fit the blade. Loosen the back clamp. Adjust the frame until ⅛" of the end of the blade is inside the bottom clamp. Tighten the back clamp and double-check the measurement.

Open the bottom clamp. Resting the peg at the top of the frame on the table, lean your upper body gently against the handle. Place the end of the saw blade inside the clamp, on top of the screw **[C]**. Hold the handle with one hand and lean gently forward against it. As the frame flexes inward, the blade will move farther into the clamp. Push it in about a quarter inch. Hold the tension on the saw frame and tighten the bottom clamp. Lean back slowly.

Check that the blade is taut when plucked, with little to no flex.

TIP

As you saw, keep your fingers a safe distance from the front of the blade and always keep all of your fingers above the bench pin where you can see them.

  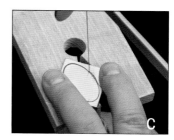

Sawing technique

The saw frame is used with a V-slot bench pin. Sit with the open end of the V pointing at your chest. The bench pin supports the metal on the legs of the V while you saw inside the gap **[A]**.

Lubricate the blade with candle wax or blade lubricant for easier sawing **[B]**.

Hold the metal with two fingers. Using one finger over each leg of the V-slot to hold with leverage takes less strength and makes it easy to turn the metal as you saw. It's OK to reach through the saw frame.

Make a notch to help you begin sawing: Place the blade against the edge of the metal and saw up and down with short strokes as if filing. Put your thumb on the smooth back of the blade to hold it steady.

To saw: Keep the blade straight up and down **[C]**. Don't angle the blade forward or back or to the side; this can cause a jam or break the blade. Saw just outside of your marked pattern; you can file away excess metal later. Relax your hand and don't press too hard; let the motion of the blade do the work.

To make a sharp turn, gently saw up and down in place, not moving forward or backward, as you turn the metal slowly so the blade faces your new direction. This will grind a wide spot in the saw cut, letting the blade move. Keep the saw moving or the blade will twist and break.

Filing

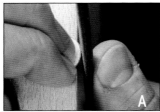

Steel files, unlike sandpaper, have rows of teeth that all slant in one direction, so it's important to file in the right direction. File forward, pushing the tip of the file away from your body. Filing backward toward the handle will not remove much metal at all.

Support your work on a V-slot bench pin. Sit directly in front of the slot, hold the metal against the wood with your fingers, and let the edge you're filing overhang the side of the pin a little. File straight up and down. Work close to the thick wood edge to help you keep the file straight **[A]**. Filing at an angle or working without support will create rough or distorted edges.

Polishing

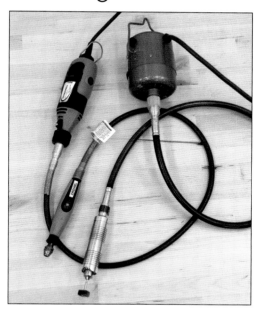

After enameling or soldering, any visible metal may be discolored with firescale. Use sandpaper or power tools to clean the metal.

Using sandpaper

The simplest way to clean your work is with files and sandpaper. Use needle files to remove excess solder or scratches. Then use a 1" (26mm) strip of 400- or 600-grit wet/dry gray silicon carbide sandpaper for metal. Sand across any scratches to remove them. To bring up a shine on your metal, burnish with a fine brass-bristle brush. Add a little hand or dish soap to the bristles, and dip the brush in water to lubricate it as you work to prevent smearing brass on the metal.

Using power tools

If you use a rotary tool such as a Dremel or a flex shaft, you need to hold the tool and your piece in a way that makes it easy to polish. I hold the tool in my right hand and

power tool safety

When using power tools, wear eye protection, tie back long hair and loose clothing, and remove rings, bracelets, and necklaces. Read and follow the manufacturer's safety directions. If anything goes wrong, turn it off. Wear a good-quality dust mask. Never wear loose-fitting gloves. Never use power tools to polish a chain or anything that can wrap around the tool without proper training.

the jewelry in my left hand. I brace my hands together with my right thumb against the fingers of my left hand. That way it's easy to stroke the wheel against the metal as I curl the fingers on my right hand, and I can control how far forward the bit moves to avoid scratching the enamel. If your arms are unsupported, you tend to have less control. Rest your hands, forearms, or elbows against a table. Adjust your chair or use a prop, like a small box, to raise your work to a comfortable height.

Use the bottom edge of the wheel
Polish with the bottom edge of the wheel. Stroke the wheel in line with its edge or across the metal with the edge of the bit at a 45-degree angle. Polishing with the face or flat plane of most wheels will break them and is harder to control.

Start in the middle and work toward you
Start with the bit in the middle of the piece and pull it toward you and off the edge. If you start on the far edge, the rotation of the tool can grab the piece and flip it out of your hand.

Sand across scratches
Sanding across a scratch will help you to see it disappear more clearly, because it will stand out against the texture you're creating. If you sand in the same direction as a scratch, it hides itself in the texture, only to reappear when polishing with finer grits. Every time you switch to a finer grit, change direction with the bit across the previous texture. Smooth the old lines completely before moving on to the next step.

Blend with even pressure and move slowly
Blend with even pressure across the surface. Don't leave dips and ripples. Move the bit slowly to give it time to rotate against the metal. Sanding and smoothing takes longer if you press too lightly or move too quickly.

Don't polish away details
Texture and details, like the shape of wire, can disappear if you use coarse abrasives such as silicone wheels. Use less pressure and don't work too long. Use fine grits that adapt to the surface, like 400-grit blue radial disks, and turn the tool so you are polishing in the same direction as any texture, not across it.

Recommended polishing abrasives
Polishing can be very messy. The dust from felt and bristle wheels charged with polishing compounds such as rouge can stain your table, floors, and clothing. Split mandrels with sandpaper and abrasives, like silicone polishing wheels, radial disks, and pin polishers, leave less dust and debris to clean up. They come in progressively finer grits that you can use to polish jewelry to a mirror shine.

Split mandrels and sandpaper

Cut sandpaper into 1x4" (26x100mm) strips. Mount the mandrel in the chuck, with the base as close to the teeth as possible. For a right-handed person, thread the paper into the slot with the abrasive side facing you. The short end should be to the right of the tool and curled over slightly. When turned on low speed, the paper will curl around the bit. Press it down against the metal until it forms a tight drum.

Silicone polishing wheels

Silicone polishers come in large and small wheels and cylinders to polish outside and inside rings, for example. Wheels are available with flat edges for flat surfaces, or knife edges to get into detailed areas. The coarse and medium wheels will remove metal and excess solder, and they can polish away details, like hammer marks and texture. They come without mandrels and have to be mounted on screw mandrels to use with your power tool. It doesn't matter which direction you mount them.

Radial bristle disks

These flexible bristles can remove firescale and polish flat surfaces, wire, and texture to a beautiful finish. Stack 3–6 disks on a screw mandrel with the curve of the bristles facing in the direction of the rotation of your tool. If they are facing the wrong way, they will bend backwards and won't work as well. If you're using the power tool in your right hand, stack the disks with the "3M" stamp facing down. The disks are expensive, but they are clean to work with and long-lasting.

Polishing pins

Thin cylinders of polishing abrasive fit into specially made mandrels that hold them securely in your rotary tool. Load the mandrel into your chuck. Then open the chuck on the mandrel to insert, remove, raise, or lower the pin.

Use flexible blue wheels to polish near enamels, since they won't harm the glass.

ENAMELING & METALWORK
Toolkits

To help you prepare for making the jewelry, review these lists. Assemble the basic kits and add extra tools as you advance through the projects. Most projects call for the basic enameling toolkit plus a few additional tools and supplies, which are listed in the box at the start of each project.

Basic enameling toolkit
- tile
- kiln brick
- large-flame butane torch
- butane fuel
- medium sifter
- small sifter
- line sifter
- 1–3 small 3-point trivets
- particle mask
- eye protection
- pennies for sifting pedestals
- glossy magazine pages for sifting
- awl
- small brush for cleaning sifter
- steel bentnose tweezers
- palette knife
- indelible marker
- screw-down punch
- holding agent (travel-size hairspray or a Preval sprayer for Klyr-Fire/water mix)
- pickle and/or Penny Brite
- emery board
- wet/dry sandpaper assortment (180–600 grit)
- enamels (lead-free opaque and transparent colors)
- counterenamel

Additional enamel tools
- tripod with screen
- Blazer butane torch
- fine-tip sable or watercolor brushes
- alundum stone
- glass brush
- cross-locking tweezers
- wet-packing tool

Sgraffito tools
- pencil and eraser
- assortment of tools for drawing lines, such as fine-tip paintbrush, awl, bamboo skewer, dental pick, and clay-shaper

Stencil tools
- stencils
- cardstock
- scissors
- fine-tip sable or watercolor paintbrush
- fine-tip rubber-tip clay shaper

Stamping tools
- VersaMark watermark stamp pad (clear)
- assorted rubber stamps
- fine-tip sable or watercolor paintbrush

Soldering toolkit
- butane torch
- butane fuel
- ceramic tile
- solder board
- charcoal block
- easy, medium, and hard solder
- eutectic solder
- flux
- flux applicator brush
- titanium solder pick
- soldering tweezers
- bowl for quenching
- safety glasses
- pickle solution in warmer pot

Basic metalwork toolkit
- rawhide mallet
- bench pin
- steel bench block with base/pad
- French shears
- jeweler's saw
- saw blades
- third hand
- ring clamp
- polished goldsmith's hammer

Additional metalwork tools & supplies
- drill press, rotary tool, or flex shaft and assortment of bits
- 2-cut half-round hand file
- needle files
- 400-grit micron-graded polishing paper
- automatic center punch
- prong pusher
- burnisher
- ball-peen hammer
- cross-peen hammer
- texture hammer
- roundnose pliers
- chainnose pliers
- flush wire cutters
- large multisize forming pliers
- half-round pliers
- ring mandrel
- dimple pliers
- center punch
- scrap wood
- wood dapping set
- steel dapping set
- dull butter knife
- patina solution
- polishing pads
- U-channel hardwood block

Projects

The progression of techniques in this section
will give you hands-on experience to build
your confidence with enameling. Each project
includes my suggestions for enamel colors, but
you can bring your own creativity to every piece
with color choices that reflect your style.

Multidangle Earri

This simple project uses light and comforta
to make a pair of earrings—a great start fo
enamel. Using opaque enamels is a great
changes as the enamel fuses.

materials
- 24-gauge copper disks: ⅞" (22mm), ¾"
  (19mm), ½" (15mm), 2 ea.
- pair of vintage-brass earring wires
- 6mm OD vintage-brass jump rings, 4
- 1319 Bitter
- 1510 Ozone
- 1915 Dove

tools & supplies
- basic enameling toolkit

48

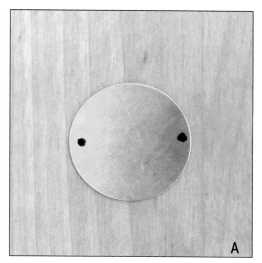

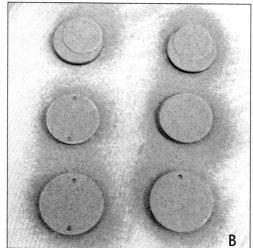

Mark and punch holes

Mark where to punch the holes on each disk with an indelible marker **[A]**. Punch the holes on each of the six disks with the screw-down metal punch. Catch the dots as they fall out of the punch and save them for later projects.

Clean the copper disks

Clean each copper piece by pickling or scrubbing with Penny Brite cleaner. Rinse and dry the pieces.

Prepare your sifting area

Cut a piece of magazine paper to fit inside a small tray. Place the tray off to one side of the tile with the kiln brick. To make it easier to pick up your disks after sifting, use pedestals made of pennies to raise them, leaving an open space under the disk.

Sift on a coat of counterenamel

Place each disk on a pedestal with the top hole at 12 o'clock. (Knowing where the hole is will help you find it again if it gets filled with enamel.) Sift an even coat of counterenamel onto the back of the disk. You can sift all the pieces at one time **[B]**.

Clean any enamels off the penny pedestals between siftings, washing them when necessary. Use the magazine paper to transfer any uncontaminated enamels back into their containers, and change sheets between colors. Mixed colors are perfect to use as counterenamel, so create a container labeled counterenamel and put any mixed colors into it.

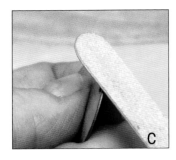

Fire the counterenamel

Place the first sifted disk on a trivet, close to the edge of the kiln brick. Fire to a glossy coat with the butane torch. Turn off the torch, wait a few seconds, and using tweezers, gently move the piece to the side of the brick to cool off.

The color will appear dark and muddy when hot, but it will change to its true color as it cools off. Counterenamel all six disks.

Using an emery board, sand the edges of the disks **[C]**. This will help the enamel flow more evenly. After you have counterenameled all six disks, clean the copper sides that were exposed to the flame.

Sift and fire the base coats

This step offers the perfect opportunity to collect counterenamel because you will be sifting multiple colors. The sifting can be done all on one piece of paper, or, if you do not want to mix the colors, place each pair of disks on their own magazine sheet. After sifting the base coat, transfer again to a trivet, fire, and let cool. If you have two trivets, fire each pair at the same time **[D]**.

After the enamel cools, repeat the process once or twice. Two coats will give the piece an even look and the color will be more saturated. Three coats will create a slightly domed effect.

Finishing

After all of the pieces are completed, check each piece to make sure there are no sharp edges. If there are, use 400-grit microngraded polishing paper to gently sand them down. 400-grit wet/dry sandpaper will also work, but it's more coarse and not as supple as the polishing paper. Use an emery board to bring the shine back to the copper edges. Connect the disks using jump rings and add earring wires **[E]**.

Holey Pod Earrings

Use shears and a drill to make custom shapes. Learn how to fire from below on a tripod for best results.

materials
- 22-gauge copper sheet, 2" (51mm) square
- pair of earring wires
- 1880 Flame Red

tools & supplies
- basic enameling toolkit
- metal shears
- drill press, flex shaft, or rotary tool
- center punch
- tripod with mesh screen

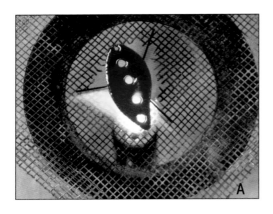

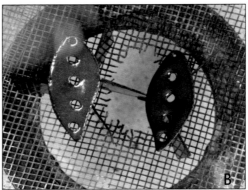

Cut and file the shapes

Draw the pods directly onto the metal with an indelible marker. Cut them out with metal shears. File the edges clean.

Drill the holes

Mark the hole locations, including a hole at the top of each piece for the earring wire. Center-punch and drill each hole. Use an awl or mini round file to clean the holes if any bits of metal remain.

Sand and clean

Sand both sides of each pod with 320-grit wet/dry sandpaper. Pickle or scrub, rinse, and dry.

Counterenamel both pods

I recommend using a counterenamel that is a mix of the colors used for the top coats. You can fire on a kiln brick as usual or use the tripod you'll use to fire the top coats of enamel.

Clean the metal

After firing, clean the darkened metal, rinse, and dry.

Fire the base coats

Sift on the base coat and fire again from below, making sure the enamel goes through all the stages to glossy [A]. Let the piece cool and watch the color change from dark back to vibrant red [B]. Repeat for the second pod.

Add second coats and finish

If desired, sift second coats of the same color, or add another color lightly sifted on the top, and fire. Repeat for both earrings. Clean the edges with an emery board or sandpaper. Add earring wires to finish the earrings.

TIP

Use a tripod whenever enameling anything that has large holes. Heating from below instead of from the side, like on the kiln brick, avoids any dark spots on the front.

Kinetic Washers Necklace

It can be challenging to come up with designs for enamel pieces. How do you connect them to use as jewelry? This necklace uses a wrapped-wire connection to combine different sizes of enameled washers.

materials
- 24-gauge copper washers, assorted sizes
- 22-gauge copper wire, 6" (15cm) per connection
- copper chain, 16" (41cm)
- clasp
- 1319 Bitter
- 1860 Flame Orange
- 1425 Sapphire

tools & supplies
- basic enameling toolkit
- tripod and mesh screen
- wire cutters
- chainnose pliers

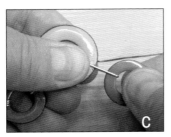

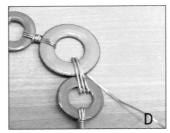

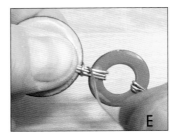

Clean

Clean all the washers, rinse, and dry.

Counterenamel all the washers and allow to cool: Sift all the washers at once on a sheet of magazine on separate pennies and have them ready to fire. Then return the enamel to its container and lay down a new piece of magazine with clean pennies for the base coat. Fire on a trivet on top of a tripod to avoid any dark spots on the surface of the enamel [A].

Clean all the washers again, rinse, and dry well.

Fire the base coat

If you are using multiple colors, this is a good time to sift them all on the same sheet and collect the enamel to use as counterenamel. Fire the base coat on all of the washers. Allow to cool.

Fire a second coat

Firing a second coat of the same color will create a more-even enameled surface and the color will be more saturated. Add a design using a stamp or stencil, if desired.

Arrange the washers

Place the fired washers on the table and position them in different arrangements until you are satisfied [B]. Draw a reference sketch to remind you of the arrangement, although you may decide to change the design as you connect the washers.

Cut the wire

Cut 6" (15cm) of 22-gauge half-round wire for each connection you will make.

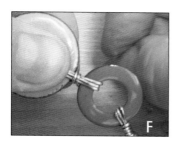

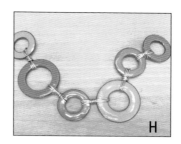

Connect the washers

Begin by connecting two washers together. Fold one end of the 6" piece of wire over the front of the first washer, bring it to the back, and rest it midway on the second washer. Keep the two washers separated with your fingers, leaving a ⅛" (3mm) gap as you wrap the wire through both washers **[C]**. Wrap 2–5 times in neat rows, holding tightly so the washers maintain their distance, and then pull the tail tightly around to the front of the washers **[D]**. Be sure the half-round side of the wire is facing out and the flat side will lie against the wire to wrap. Wrap around all the wires and fill the gap between the two washers **[E]**. Keep the wraps tight **[F]**. Bring the tail to the back, and tuck it into one or more of the wraps so it does not dislodge or cause scratching **[G]**.

Repeat

Continue connecting all of the washers, following the steps above. As you add connections, play with the design to make sure it lies as you want it to **[H]**. Adjust as you go along to construct the exact design you want. After all the connections have been made, if you are not satisfied, you can loosen the wire slightly by moving the washers a bit and rearranging their positions. Squeeze the wraps to tighten again. If you want the washers to move as you wear the necklace, do not tighten too much.

Add patina

Add patina to the wire if desired: Brush on some cold liver of sulfur or silver black, wait 5–10 minutes, neutralize, rinse, and dry. With a polishing pad, rub off as much patina as you like, leaving some in the crevices.

Add chain

Cut the chain in half. Wrap a connection as above between each end washer and the chain ends. Attach half of the clasp to each end.

Stenciled Pendant

Use stencils to create patterns as you sift! Lots of materials can be used to make stencils. You can cut your own from paper or use found objects—open-weave rubber placemats or wire mesh make interesting patterns, or try laser-pierced greeting cards or metal filigree.

materials
- 24-gauge copper sheet, 1⅛" (29mm) square
- 1430 Spruce
- 1830 Marigold
- 1995 Black

tools & supplies
- basic enameling toolkit
- stencil
- fine-tip paintbrush

Punch holes and clean

Punch a hole in two corners of the square. Clean the metal.

Counterenamel and clean

Counterenamel the back of the piece, allow to cool, and clean off the firescale.

Fire the base coat

Sift a base coat on the front. I used spruce, but any opaque color that will contrast with the colors you have chosen for the dots will be perfect.

Place the stencil

Once you have the base coat fired and cooled off, place it on top of the stack of pennies in your sifting area. Lay the stencil on top, or hold it just above the surface with tweezers. This stencil was made by punching holes in a piece of cardstock.

Sift the first color

Fill the sifter about one third of the way with the first color and sift it over half of the stencil. Place the stencil on top or hold it just above the surface with your fingers or tweezers [A]. Quickly bring the stencil straight up and over to the side, away from the piece so the grains fall off away from the piece. Put any unused

enamel back in the container and clean out the sifter.

Sift the second color

Sift the second color over the other half of the piece, then lift off the stencil with tweezers. Remove stray grains of enamel using a fine-tip paintbrush, if desired, or keep them as part of the design.

Fire the enamel

Use a trivet and kiln brick to fire the enamel [B]. Stop firing as soon as the piece reaches the glossy stage, and allow to cool.

TIP

Firing stages change quickly, but they take longer with multiple layers of enamel or with thick-gauge metal. Be patient.

more fun with stencils

Stencils are a great way to add interest to any enameled piece. Many found objects can be used as stencils. Mass-produced stencils are available in craft shops. Gift shops often carry cards with laser-cut designs, and bead stores usually have large metal or plastic charms with cutout designs that can make clever stencil designs.

It is also easy to cut out your own designs from cardstock with a craft knife, or use just the edge of a sheet of paper. Use fancy scissors to make beautifully scalloped or serrated edges, or mask pieces with painter's tape. Leaves and other organic materials make great designs to sift around too. Use craft punches to create a design or try using a rubber placemat with a web-like design. Remember that the negative space will create the positive enamel shapes.

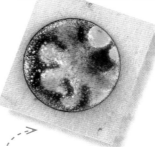

multilayer transparent

When multiple layers of enamel are added in multiple firings, the colors take on greater dimension and depth. Begin by sifting light-color transparents over white. Add darker colors in subsequent layers.

raised dots stencil

I sifted enamel through holes in a rubber placemat and used more enamel than usual to build up and add height and texture to this design. The disk on the left was sifted over clean copper, so after firing, the firescale shows as a design element.

stencil with wire mesh: hammered silver earrings

Make simple yet eye-catching earrings using wire mesh as a stencil. Choosing two colors that are close in value produces a subtle effect. Make holes in the disks, counterenamel, and fire on a base coat. Hold the wire mesh at an angle and sift a new color on, remove the stencil, and place the piece on a trivet. Fire just until you see the first signs of glossy; if you fire too long, the design can disappear.

Hammer the silver disks with a pattern that mimics the pattern of the wire mesh. Punch a hole and add patina, if desired. Hang on your favorite earring wires.

stencil with metal:
mirror-image mod earrings

It's easy to use any copper shape to fabricate a stunning pair of patterned earrings. I used an oval, but any shape will work. Counterenamel and clean the disks, and fire a base coat on the top. Place the metal you are using for a stencil and sift on a color. Remove the stencil and clean up any excess enamel with a fine-tip brush. Fire the piece, allow to cool, sift the next color, and repeat. Continue until you have the pattern you want. Over the fired enamel, sift a circle with a new contrasting color and fire. After the enamel is cool, use a straw or line sifter to add a final dot and fire. If you add the dot on top of the sifted circle and fire those together, color will bleed and the shapes will not be as well-defined.

flecks or no flecks?

When you use a stencil, sometimes small flecks (grains of enamel) will remain around the main shapes. It's your choice to clean them off for a crisp finish or leave them to become part of the background design (which I often do).

If you like a neat look, clean the top using a very fine-tip paintbrush or a rubber clay-shaping tool. Carefully push or brush each unwanted fleck from the center off the edge of the metal.

adding dimension

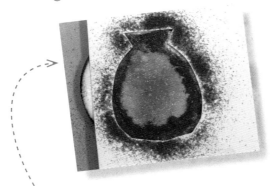

Create shading and dimension: Sift one color over the entire opening, fire, and sift a darker color around the edges for the second firing.

Have a small, flat shape such as a scrapbooking cutout you like? Glue a stick to it and sift around it.

Stamped Dog Tag

Use watermark stamp ink and any rubber stamp image or alphabet letters to create an enameled design. The sifted enamels will stick to the ink.

materials
- 24-gauge copper dog tag blank
- 1319 Bitter
- 1940 Steel
- 1995 Black

tools & supplies
- basic enameling toolkit
- rubber stamps
- VersaMark watermark stamp pad
- fine-tip paintbrush

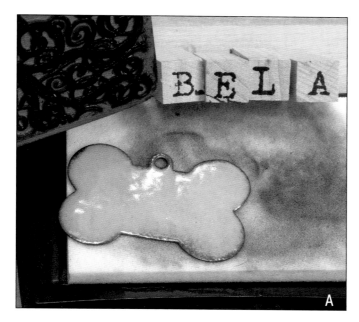

A

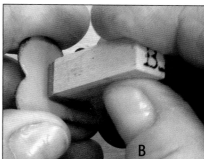

B

Prepare the metal
Clean, counterenamel, and remove any firescale from the copper dog tag.

Fire a base coat
Choose the colors for the base coat and what stamp to use. It is important to have a good contrast so the stamp really shows up, or it will just be a faint glimmer on the glass. Light colors work well for the base, and black is a good choice for the stamp. If you want a dark background, then white will be the best bet for the stamp. If the enamel on the base coat is uneven, it might be difficult to get a flush coat of ink, so fire another coat to smooth it before stamping.

Design the tag
Pick out the stamps that you will use and decide on placement of the stamps **[A]**.

Ink the enamel
The VersaMark ink is especially good at adhering to fired enamels and for holding onto sifted enamels. Coat the stamp with ink and bring the metal to the stamp, pressing firmly enough to transfer the image **[B]**. Be careful if you place the enameled piece on the table and then stamp it; stamping directly on the enamel too hard against the table can crack it. If you are using several stamps on one piece, fire the enamel between stampings.

TIP
The enamel must be flat and even; lumps make for uneven stamping. If the stamp slips while inking, remove the ink with rubbing alcohol, rinse, and dry. Sand the enamel so it has some tooth and stamp again.

take some time to experiment
A great way to learn about how enamel colors fire and look when combined is to make a series of similar designs and experiment with small changes and different combinations of color. I suggest stopping at different stages and checking out the piece. You can always go back and fire to the final stage.

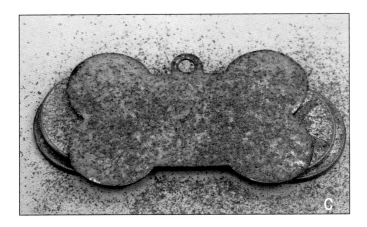

TIP

Begin slowly by heating the kiln brick and then the trivet. Finally, aim the flame under the enameled piece as soon as you see a change in color. Heating slowly will reduce the chance of enamel popping off the ink.

Sift over the inked design

Sift the enamel over the stamped area right away, before it has a chance to dry or smear **[C]**.

Remove the excess enamel

Turn the piece to its side and gently tap it against the magazine page. As you tap, excess grains will fall off and the enamel powder will stick to just the ink. There's usually a dusty halo of color around the design, which can create a pretty effect after firing. If you prefer, use a fine-tip brush or clay shaping tool to remove excess enamel.

Fire

Transfer the dog tag to the trivet and fire. Watch as the design is revealed. This is fun to see because the changes in the stamped enamel are more dramatic than a basic enamel coat.

You may see fumes rising as the ink dries; be sure to wear a mask and eye protection when you fire. Allow to cool.

Clean the edges. Sand off any sharp edges with 600-grit wet/dry sandpaper.

Add a new stamp or color

Repeat the entire process with new stamps or colors to complete your dog tag design.

Three-Toned Twins

The best way to see what a transparent color looks like is to experiment with it over a variety of surfaces: clean metal, clear enamel, or a color. Making these earrings using a wide range of colors over bare metal and a white base coat will give you solid information on how the colors react—and you'll have some lovely earrings when you're done with your tests.

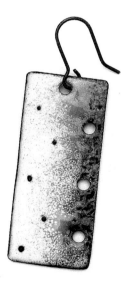

materials
- 24-gauge copper sheet, 2" (51mm) square
- pair of earring wires
- 1010 Undercoat (white)
- 2530 Water

tools & supplies
- basic enameling toolkit
- screw-down punch
- dimple pliers, 1mm
- medium-cut file
- 220- and 400-grit wet/dry sandpaper
- indelible marker
- metal shears
- steel bench block
- rawhide mallet

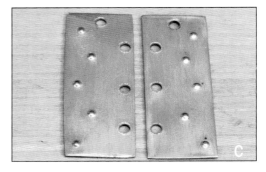

Cut copper rectangles

Measure two rectangles on the metal ⅝ x1½" (16x38mm), mark them with indelible marker, and cut them out using metal shears. If they are slightly uneven, don't worry—they can be filed to be exact or left uneven.

Flatten the sheet

Using shears to cut metal can cause the metal to curve, so if this happens, place the metal with the convex side face down on the steel bench block and hit it with the rawhide mallet until it is flat.

File and sand the shapes

File the edges and soften the corners if you like by gently filing them down. Using 220- and 400-grit sandpaper, smooth all the edges and the front and back of both rectangles.

Mark the metal

Mark the rectangles with dots to indicate where the raised dots will go, and mark circles for punching holes **[A]**. Don't forget to mark holes for the earring wires as well!

Punch holes and dimple dots

With the larger of the two punches on the screw-down punch, make all the holes. Use dimple pliers to create the raised dots **[B].** The raised side of the jaws will indent the metal, so the opposite side will have raised dots.

Clean, rinse, and dry

Clean both pieces. They should be mirror images of each other so they sit well as earrings **[C].**

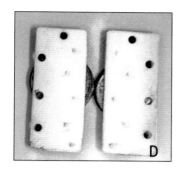

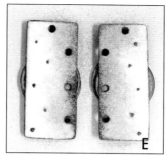

Counterenamel

Sift a counterenamel color. I used a mix of colors that included the transparent color I will use on the front. Blend some opaque and transparent colors in a container, cover, and shake to mix it all up. Fire.

Clean, rinse and dry.

Add a base coat

Sift a light coat of white from the center to the dimple side of the rectangles **[D]**. If the dimples are completely covered, you can brush the enamel off the top carefully onto the lower surface so the dots will be metal when fired. If you don't like that look, just leave the enamel on the dots.

Fire

Fire both rectangles. Allow to cool.

Add color

Sift a light coat of water blue over the other side of the rectangle, covering some of the white **[E]**.

Fire and finish

Fire both pieces and allow to cool. Now you will see how the transparent color looks over clean copper and over the white. Add an earring wire to each piece.

TIP

Play with different shapes and create your own designs while you experiment with the colors you have.

Foldformed Leaf Pendant

Handmade leaves in all shapes
and sizes are always beautiful.
This project demonstrates how to
make a lovely line fold and create
a varied, textured surface for
enameling. Experiment with both
opaque and transparent enamel to
create vivid or muted leaves.

materials
- 24-gauge copper sheet, 1½ x2" (38x51mm)
- 2030 Medium Fusing Clear
- 2240 Olive
- 2840 Mandarin Orange
- 2330 Avocado
- 2220 Chartreuse

tools & supplies
- basic enameling toolkit
- rawhide mallet
- goldsmith's or planishing hammer
- dull butter knife
- auto center punch
- dimple pliers: 3mm, 4mm, or 7mm (optional)
- steel bench block
- bench pin
- 320-grit wet/dry sandpaper

TIP Dimple pliers produce nice
textures of hills and valleys. Use one size
or a variety in this leaf project. These pliers
can also be used to create ruffles on the
edges of thin-gauge metals.

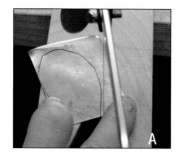
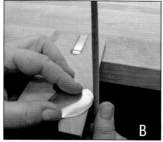
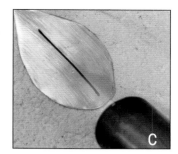
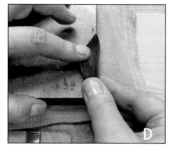

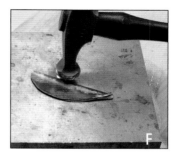

Create the leaf shape

Draw a leaf shape directly onto the copper with an indelible marker and saw it out **[A]**. Using the bench pin as a work surface **[B]**, file the edges to refine the shape and sand the leaf, including the edges, with 320-grit wet/dry sandpaper.

Anneal

In order to easily fold and form the line down the middle of the leaf, anneal it so it's soft and malleable. Draw a marker line on the metal, place it on a kiln brick, and heat it with the torch **[C]**. When the line disappears and the metal turns a light red, keep heating for 30 more seconds, quench it in water, and dry. I usually wait to pickle the metal until it's ready to texture, because I will have to anneal it again.

Fold the leaf

Place the leaf on a square steel bench block, with the centerline on the edge. Use a mallet to fold half of the leaf over the edge **[D]**. Place the partially folded leaf on the bench block and use the mallet to finish folding it **[E]**. For a tighter, more defined fold line, strike it with a polished hammer to planish the fold **[F]**. To make a line texture on the fold, move the leaf to the edge of the block and use the narrow wedge of a goldsmith's hammer. Be careful to hit the metal and not to ding your hammer! Flip it over and repeat on the other side.

Anneal again

The metal is work-hardened now. Anneal it again to soften it.

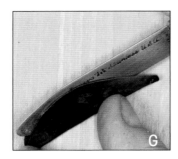

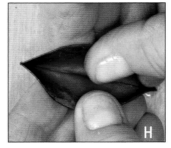

TIP If you don't have a dull butter knife and the metal is soft enough, use an awl to carefully separate the metal and then continue opening with your fingers.

Open the fold

Use a dull butter knife to open the fold carefully **[G]**. Open it wide enough to grasp both sides with your fingers. Continue to open it until it won't go any farther **[H]**. Place it on the steel bench block with the opening of the fold up. Gently mallet each side down until they touch the steel. Then mallet the entire crease to flatten it completely.

Clean and add texture

Clean the metal. Add texture using a variety of hammers on a steel bench block and one of my favorite tools, the auto center punch. The auto center punch makes deep divots if used on a piece of scrap wood. Place the auto center punch on the metal at an angle **[I]**. Firmly press it down to make a small depression. Continue to create overall texture. Use dimple pliers to make larger impressions if desired **[J]**.

Clean the metal

Prepare the piece for enameling: Clean it again to remove oils and dirt.

Counterenamel

Because the leaf has hills and valleys, spray lightly with a holding agent (nonaerosol hairspray or a 50/50 solution of Klyr-Fire and distilled water). Sift on counterenamel, let it sit for 10–15 minutes, and fire. Allow it to cool, then clean the metal.

Apply a base coat

Spray lightly with a holding agent and sift a base coat of clear on the front. Let it sit for 10–15 minutes before firing.

Allow to cool, spray again with a holding agent, and sift multiple transparent colors in a random pattern, overlapping them slightly. Fire until glossy. Repeat the sifting and firing if you want more depth of color or until you are satisfied with the look.

Dots, Dots, Dots Pendant

Make your own small copper dots for an eye-catching pendant. (Fine-silver and brass dots work also.) Vary the gauge of the dots for interesting textures. You'll also learn how to make a enameled headpin.

materials
- copper dots collected from making holes in copper disks, various sizes and gauges
- 16-gauge round copper wire, 5" (13cm)
- 18-gauge round copper wire, 5" (13cm)
- 1" (26mm) diameter 24-gauge copper disk
- copper jump ring
- 2530 Water
- 1520 Calamine
- 1360 Jungle
- 2030 Medium Fusing Clear or 1010 Undercoat (white)

tools & supplies
- basic enameling toolkit
- tripod and screen
- ring mandrel
- goldsmith's hammer
- rawhide mallet
- cross-locking tweezers
- steel bench block
- screw-down punch

Prepare the enamels for dipping

You'll make enameled headpins by first balling up the wire and then immersing them in enamel while hot. Open a few containers of enamel and set them on the tile in front of you. For this technique, some colors work better than others. Using undercoat white as the first coat helps to bring out the color. Calamine blue and jungle green work well. Transparent colors can be a bit muted if fired directly on the copper, but will often look better if fired over a first coat of clear or undercoat. Experiment with a few headpins, trying different colors, to see how they look after firing.

Ball both ends of the wire

Cut 5" (13cm) of 18-gauge round copper wire. Hold it in the middle with cross-locking tweezers. Place it on the tile and light the torch. Hold the torch steady with your nondominant hand, and pick up the tweezers. Work over the tile and hold the wire straight up and down. Dip the bottom end of the wire into the flame, just in front of the tip of the blue cone. The wire end will glow bright red and then ball up [A]. Stop when the ball reaches the size you want. Flip the wire over and repeat. Quench in water.

Add enamel to the balls

Hold the balled end of the wire in front of the tip of the blue cone inside the flame, heat it to a bright orange, and dip it right away into the enamel to coat it with enamel powder. Remove from the enamel and fire to glossy. Repeat the process, heating, dipping, and firing three or four times until satisfied [B]. I used a bent screen to raise the headpins and prevent contamination as they cooled [C]. Dipping them into vermiculite or carefully resting them on the tile after a few moments also works.

Punch a hole

Punch a hole in the disk.

Clean the metal

Clean, rinse, and dry the disk.

Counterenamel

Counterenamel the disk, clean off any firescale, rinse well, and dry.

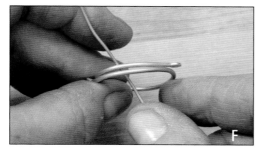

Fire a base coat

Use clear as the base coat, fire, and cool.

Add second coat and dots

Place the copper dots in a clean dish for easy access **[D]**. Sift on a light coat of clear or spray on a light coat of holding agent to prevent the dots from sliding off the glossy surface. Arrange the dots on the disk and allow to dry if you used a holding agent.

Fire the disk

Fire slowly, heating first on the kiln brick, then the trivet, and finally directly under the metal until the enamel is glossy orange. The dots will now be embedded in the enamel.

Check the results

The color will have darkened in some areas and remained copper-colored in others. The raised copper dots can be left dark or cleaned by sanding or pickling. If you want to add a bit more color, sift on a light coat, carefully brushing off any excess enamel grains on the dots, and fire again.

Make a ring with ball ends

Ball up both ends of the 16-gauge wire. Make sure your torch is full because 16-gauge will take longer to ball up than 18-gauge wire. Quench and dry. The balls can be left round or flattened. Flatten them one at a time on the bench block with a polished goldsmith's hammer **[E]**.

Clean the edges

File the edges if they're sharp and sand off any burrs with 320-grit sandpaper.

Shape the ring

Bend the wire around a ring mandrel, crossing the two ends past each other, and curving down the sides. Join the wire where it is doubled by wrapping it with one of the double enameled headpins **[F]**. Adjust the enameled balls so they stand up.

Work-harden the link

With a goldsmith's hammer, flatten the wire loop to harden it so it keeps its shape, avoiding the headpins **[G]**. Connect the disk to the ring with a jump ring.

Teardrop Dangle Earrings

Now that you've practiced your enameling skills with a few projects, try combining a few techniques and working with curved forms.

materials

- ⅝" (16mm) diameter 24-gauge copper disks, 2

- ¾" (19mm) diameter 24-gauge copper teardrop shapes, 2

- 20-gauge fine-silver wire, 4" (10cm)

- 2520 Aqua

- 1510 Ozone

- 1319 Bitter

tools & supplies

- basic enameling toolkit

- dapping set

- screw-down punch

- indelible marker

- cross-locking tweezers

- steel bench block

- riveting or cross-peen hammer

- 320-grit wet/dry sandpaper

Enamel the fine-silver headpins

Use fine-silver wire and a transparent enamel color to make two balled-end headpins to connect the two copper pieces and also become the earring wires: Cut two 2" (51mm) lengths of fine-silver wire and make two headpins with enamel balls on the end (see Dots, Dots, Dots Pendant, p. 69).

Ball and dip each wire in the enamel three times. When done firing, hold it in the cross-locking tweezers for 30 seconds before releasing, so the enamel keeps its shape and has time to cool a bit. Then place it on the ceramic tile and let it cool completely.

Punch holes

Mark the center of the disk and the top of the teardrop shape to indicate where you will punch holes. Punch out all the holes. Sand the front and back with 320-grit wet/dry sandpaper to remove any burrs from the punch.

Dap the disk

Dap the disks slightly. It's always a good idea to make sure all the parts have holes and are ready to go before enameling **[A]**.

Clean the copper

Clean all the copper pieces, rinse well, and dry.

Counterenamel

I used a combination of blues as my counterenamel for both shapes. Counter-enamel the teardrops and allow to cool.

Use a holding agent so the enamel adheres to the disks. Spray a light coat onto the exterior and then sift enamel over it. Holding the disk with a skewer through the hole allows for the best coverage **[B]**. Transfer each disk from the skewer to the trivet by lifting it gently with your fingers and placing it carefully onto the trivet. Let both disks dry for 20–30 minutes, fire, and allow to cool.

Clean

Clean the metal, rinse, and dry.

Fire the base coats

Sift a base coat on all the pieces. For the disks, make sure that after you spray the holding agent, you tap any of the excess out of the interior so the enamel does not pool at the center when sifted. Fire. Allow to cool.

TIP

Fine silver balls up much faster than copper, so if the flame is too intense, the ball can fall off. Use a small flame and don't apply too much heat too quickly, and watch for signs of trouble, like glossy surfaces in the wrong section of the wire or seeing the ball quiver or boil. As soon as the end glows, dip it in the enamel powder and raise it to the flame again. You can always pull the flame away for a moment if it seems too intense.

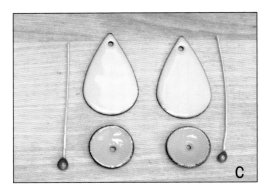

TIP
Fire a second coat for a more even surface interest. Sifting a contrasting color or using a stencil to add a touch of another color are great options.

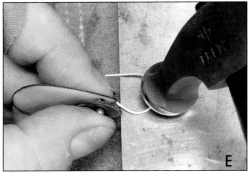

Attach the pieces
Now that all the pieces are enameled **[C]**, string the headpin through the disk and the teardrop.

Make the earring wires
Bend the wire over a mandrel that is a good size for the earring wire **[D]**, and bend it back toward the front of the earring so the curve is just over the metal shapes. This will help the earring hang just right. Form both earring wires at the same time so they're identical.

Harden the wire
Hold the earring wire on the steel bench block. With a polished riveting hammer or cross-peen hammer, strike the curve of the wire to flatten it slightly **[E]**. This will also harden the wire and help it keep its shape. Use a wire rounder or cup bur to smooth the end of the wire. Repeat for the other earring.

Buds on a Vine Necklace

This project expands on the technique for making enameled headpins that you learned in the Dots, Dots, Dots Pendant project. The headpins are wrapped around forged 12-gauge copper wire.

materials
- 12-gauge copper wire, 9" (23cm)
- 16-gauge copper wire:
  4" (10cm) piece
  3½" (89mm) piece
  2" (51mm) pieces, 2
- 18-gauge copper wire:
  3" (76mm) pieces, 5
  2" pieces, 2
- 6mm jump rings, 3
- copper chain, 12" (31cm)
- clasp
- 2030 Medium Clear Fusing
- 1010 Undercoat (white)
- 1520 Calamine
- 1830 Marigold
- 1319 Bitter
- 2530 Water
- 1870 Orient
- 1760 Iris

tools & supplies
- basic enameling toolkit
- cross-peen hammer
- screw-down punch
- steel bench block
- cross-locking tweezers
- roundnose pliers

A

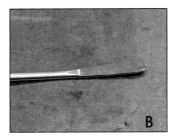

B

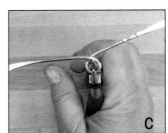

C

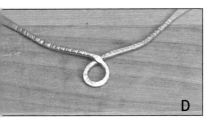

D

E

F

TIP

Enamel may chip off during wrapping. Work over paper to catch any glass chips. Handle carefully. Collect the shards to add texture to other enamel pieces or simply discard them.

Make enameled headpins

Cut the lengths needed for the headpins (listed on p. 75) from 16- and 18-gauge copper wire. Ball both ends of each wire and enamel the ends (see the Dots, Dots, Dots Pendant, p. 69). If you have extra wire, make more enameled headpins for future projects. Allow to cool. Clean the stems **[A]**.

Forge and prepare the vine

Cut 6" (15cm) of 12-gauge copper wire. Use a polished cross-peen hammer on a steel bench block to flatten each end into a paddle shape **[B]**. Holding the wire with roundnose pliers at its mid-point, bend the ends with your fingers to form a loop **[C]**. Rest the loop on the bench block, and hammer it to flatten it and to work-harden it. Refine and round the ends of the wire with a hand file. Mark and punch a hole in each of the ends. Smooth the ends. Use the wedge of the hammer to texture the wire **[D]**.

Wrap the buds

This next part of the necklace is more freeform. Wrap one of the double-ended enameled headpins around a section of the 12-gauge vine **[E]**. Wrap just tightly enough to keep the buds in place, but not too tightly—you might crack the enamel. Coil more enameled headpins around the vine, making a pretty pattern of buds **[F]**.

Make the link

Make a smaller, straight version of the vine without the loop: Using 3" (76mm) of 12-gauge wire, forge the ends, punch holes, and texture. Wrap buds around it to match the centerpiece. Connect the vine sections to each other.

Cut the chain in half. Connect the ends of the vine section to one end of each chain with jump rings. Attach half of the clasp to the remaining chain ends.

Shimmer Earrings

These glistening earrings are made with fine-silver sheet, transparent enamels, and silver foil. The enamel is luminescent over the silver, and the foil adds intriguing texture.

materials
- silver foil, 1" (26mm) square
- 22-gauge fine-silver sheet, 1" square
- pair of earring wires
- 2020 Clear for Silver
- 2220 Chartreuse
- 2435 Turquoise
- 2430 Beryl

tools & supplies
- basic enameling toolkit
- awl or steel brush
- fine-tip paintbrush
- clean water
- sharp scissors
- Blazer torch

TIP

Use the Blazer torch to fire these earrings. The Blazer has a smaller flame than the large-flame torch. Fine-silver has a lower melting point than copper, so it is safer to use a smaller flame that can apply focused, less-intense heat. Note that this project calls for Thompson's 2020 Clear for Silver, which is designed for best results with silver.

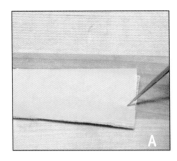
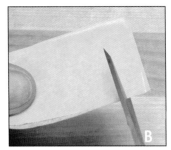
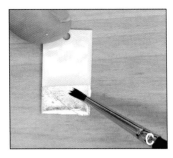

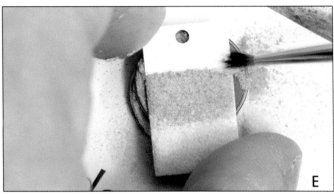

TIP

Cut and clean the metal

Cut two 1x½" (26x13mm) pieces of fine-silver sheet and punch holes at the top of each rectangle. File and sand the edges. Clean and dry the metal.

Counterenamel and fire the base coat

Counterenamel with a transparent enamel mix of the colors you are using on the front and allow to cool. Sift a coat of 2020 clear over the entire piece and fire. Repeat the step on the second piece and allow both pieces to cool.

Cut the silver foil

While the foil is sandwiched between two sheets of paper **[A]**, use very sharp scissors to cut two pieces to fit across the bottom of each rectangle. With the foil still inside the paper, use a beading awl or wire brush to poke fine holes in the foil **[B]**. This will help prevent air bubbles from forming under the foil

while firing. Brush a thin coat of Klyr-Fire over the rectangle where you will add the foil. Use a fine-tip paintbrush with a touch of water to pick up the foil and place it on the rectangle **[C]**. Press it to the enamel with a burnisher or the end of the brush **[D]**. Always apply silver or gold foil to a coat of enamel that has already been fired. Repeat for the second earring.

Sift and fire the final coat

Sift nile green over the foil and beryl in the center. Clean the top edge of the beryl with a brush **[E]**, and then sift chartreuse at the top. Transfer it to the trivet and fire with the Blazer torch. Start slowly, first heating the kiln brick, then the trivet, and finally directly underneath. Heating slowly when using foil will help you avoid burning it. Repeat for the other earring and allow both pieces to cool.

Add earring wires to finish the earrings.

Enameled Dish

Dap a mini dish from copper and then explore how separation enamel adds depth and texture to your designs by revealing the layers beneath.

materials
- 24-gauge copper disk, 1¼" (32mm) diameter
- Klyr-Fire
- 1010 Undercoat (white)
- 1319 Bitter
- 2530 Beryl
- 2435 Turquoise
- separation enamel powder

tools & supplies
- basic enameling toolkit
- sgraffito toolkit
- medium sifter
- ball-peen hammer
- rawhide mallet
- wood dapping set
- steel dapping punch
- steel bench block

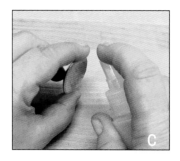

TIP
Because this dish is curved, it's not necessary to counter-enamel. Enamel the interior and keep the exterior copper.

Shape the dish

Dome the disk with a dapping block. A shallow dome is best so the dish sits level on the trivet. Make a flat bottom: Place the dome curved side down on the steel bench block. Reverse the dapping punch and center the flat end inside the dome. Using a rawhide mallet, tap the punch to make a flat spot **[A]**. The dish should sit level on your table **[B]**.

Spray and sift a base coat

Spray the inside of the dish lightly with a holding agent **[C]**. Hold the piece with your fingers and angle the dish as you sift undercoat white to cover all the edges well **[D]**. Spray a light coat of Klyr-Fire again.

Add color

Immediately sift a light coat of bitter green and let it sit for 10–15 minutes to let the Klyr-Fire dry. Transfer the dish to a trivet on top of a screen on a tripod, and fire from below. Make sure the torch is full, since this will need maximum heat to fire. Allow the dish to cool, spray the holding agent again, add a

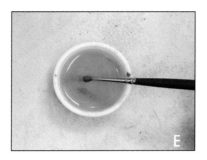

light coat of bitter green, let dry, and fire. Allow to cool, spray, sift a coat of beryl green, and let dry.

Sgraffito

Spray the holding agent, add a layer of beryl green, and let dry. Draw a few lines in the enamel with an awl to reveal some of the bitter green below, fire, and cool.

Add more color

The last layer before adding separation enamel should be a transparent color. Spray the holding agent so the enamel adheres to the dish, add a coat of transparent turquoise, let dry, and fire.

Prepare and apply the separation enamel

There are many ways to prepare separation enamel powder, such as using special oils, but you can simply mix it with a little distilled water and a touch of Klyr-Fire until it is thick and creamy. Mix a small amount in a clean container **[E]**.

With a very fine-tip brush or a bamboo skewer, apply the separation enamel in straight lines, squiggles, or dots. Make sure there are gaps between any lines **[F]**. Allow to dry thoroughly, then fire until it goes very glossy and you see the separation enamel disappear or there are other dramatic changes in the enamel that you like.

If you have two torches, keep one handy and be prepared to use them both to fire if the single torch is not creating enough heat to get results you like.

After the dish cools, check the results. You can always repeat by applying more separation enamel and firing again until you are satisfied.

using separation enamel

Separation enamel is not actually enamel, but when painted over multiple layers of a mix of opaque and transparent enamels, it will create varied indentations in the enamel to reveal some colors in all the layers. The results are not always predictable; they will depend on the thickness of the metal and the colors used.

You may get results using just one large-flame torch, but if you have a second torch, it is possible to produce amazing results. Be sure both torches are full of fuel. Light them carefully. Do not aim them at each other; point toward the bottom of the dish.

Sticks & Stones Earrings

Just like enamel, seed beads are made of glass, so they can be fired right along with your sifted color. Use beads and glass threaders to create unusual designs.

materials
- 24-gauge copper disks with 7/8" (22mm) round cutouts, 1 5/8" (41mm) diameter, 2
- seed beads, size 11 and 8, opaque yellow and yellow-green
- opaque black glass threaders
- pair of earring wires
- 1465 Peacock

tools & supplies
- basic enameling toolkit
- tripod with screen

TIP I purchased my copper blanks with offset cutouts already made. You can design your own donut shapes using a jeweler's saw or a disk cutter.

TIP Firing anything that is open like a washer this way prevents dark areas from forming on the top surface.

Punch holes and clean the metal

Punch a hanging hole in the top of each copper shape. Clean the pieces, rinse, and dry.

Counterenamel and clean

Sift on counterenamel and place the pieces on a trivet on a tripod. The tripod should be on a tile for safety. Fire to a glossy coat. Repeat for both earrings. Allow to cool. Clean, rinse, and dry.

Fire the base coat

Sift and fire on the base coat on both pieces. Repeat for a second coat if desired. Allow to cool.

Add beads and threaders

After the pieces have cooled, spray them with a holding agent to fix the glass beads and threaders in place during firing. You can also sift on a light coat of the same color (or 2030 medium fusing clear), and add the beads and threaders.

Place one piece on the trivet. Make sure it's level to prevent the beads from rolling off. Place the seed beads and threaders to make a pattern. Let the piece dry for 10 minutes before firing **[A]**.

Heat slowly

Heat from below using a medium flame, from far away. The goal is to heat the piece so it stabilizes and so the glass adheres to the surface without jumping around before the enamel fuses.

Fire to glossy and finish

Increase the flame and continue firing from below, concentrating on each segment of the trivet until the enamel goes through its stages. At the glossy stage, although the beads and threaders will look raised, they will be securely embedded in the enamel. Repeat placing beads and threaders on the second piece. Fire and allow both pieces to cool. Add earring wires to finish.

a smooth surface

For the earrings, I stopped firing as the enamel layer turned glossy. The thin threaders were slightly raised but well connected. The seed beads were raised even higher but also securely anchored. As you fire longer, the threaders and beads will melt and blend into the surface, as they did in this pendant. Fire just past the glossy stage and stop when you see the details sink into the enamel.

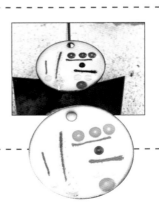

Sgraffito Tab-Set Pendant

Create a fabulous enameled cabochon by drawing directly through enamel powders to reveal the color below. Saw out a tab setting to frame your design.

materials
- 22-gauge copper sheet, 3x4" (76x100mm)
- 1995 Black
- 1319 Bitter
- 1870 Orient
- 1810 Buttercup

tools & supplies
- basic enameling toolkit
- large glass quenching bowl
- 0- or 2-cut half-round hand file
- jeweler's saw
- 2/0 saw blade
- flat mini needle file
- prong pusher
- sgraffito toolkit
- rubber cement
- leather scrap

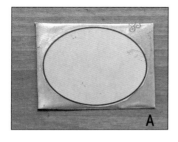

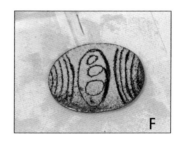

Saw out the oval

Trace or photocopy the oval from the template provided and glue it on the copper sheet using rubber cement **[A]**. Wait 10 minutes for the glue to dry before sawing.

Using a 2/0 saw blade, saw out the oval, leaving the line on the pattern intact for filing **[B]**.

File and sand

File to the lines using the hand file **[C]**. Use the file to remove excess metal and to refine the oval shape. Sand both sides and the edges with 320-grit sandpaper **[D]**.

Counterenamel and fire on a base coat

Clean, counterenamel the back, clean the metal again, and fire on a top coat of black. Allow to cool.

Sift on another color

Sift the second color (bitter green) on top. This is the sgraffito layer. If you choose a different color, make sure the colors are contrasting.

Sgraffito

Simple tools can be used to draw in the enamel: dental picks, bamboo skewers, awls, erasers, very fine-tip watercolor brushes, or even a piece of stiff wire. Each tool will take a different amount of enamel away, leaving a different line weight.

You can raise the piece on something smaller and stable to make it easier to hold the edges while drawing. Draw into the enamel **[E, F]**. Be careful not to disturb the rest of the enamel.

TIP The oval can be cut with metal shears, but it will need to be flattened with a rawhide mallet and filed more than if it was sawn.

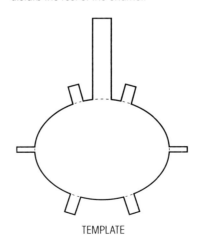

TEMPLATE

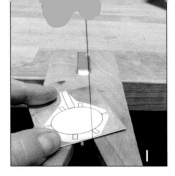

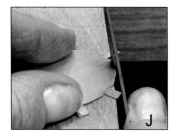

Transfer the piece to the trivet carefully and fire **[G]**. As the enamel goes through the stages of firing, watch as the pattern is revealed. Even faint or thin lines will hold after firing. Allow to cool.

Add dots

I filled the sgraffito circles with more color. With the line sifter or a narrow straw, apply the tiny dots of color **[H]**. To use the straw, put a little of the enamel color you want to add in the tip of the straw, then gently tap the straw to sift enamel where you want it to go. It's OK to sift while the metal is on the trivet if the new powder doesn't get near the trivet. Brush away any excess grains. Fire until glossy and allow to cool.

Saw out the tab setting

Glue a copy of the tab-setting template to the copper sheet and let dry for 10 minutes. Saw out the design **[I]**. Rest the metal on the bench pin and file to the pattern **[J]**. Hold the metal in a ring clamp for a firm grip. Use either side, and press the wedge into the opposite side. Tapping the wedge against the table will tighten the clamp. Brace the clamp on a bench pin. File all the edges using a

mini flat file **[K]**. Leave the tab ends flat, or file off the corners and give each tab a gentle curve with the file.

Anneal and sand

Anneal the tab setting (see the Fold-formed Leaf Pendant, p. 66). Quench, pickle for 5–10 minutes, rinse, and dry.

Sand both sides with 320-grit wet/dry sandpaper to remove any scratches. Use 600-grit to create a satin finish.

Check the fit

Place the tab setting face up on a scrap of leather and check the fit with the enameled cabochon **[L]**. The base of the setting should match the outline of the cab, with only the tabs exposed. If some of the base sticks out, use the cab as a template and mark what to file away. Sand to blend any file and work marks.

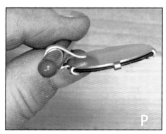 

Set the tabs

Since the metal of the tab setting is dead soft, it won't take much pressure to set the tabs. Rest the setting on the leather. Starting with the tabs near the bail, gently raise the tab with your fingers and use a prong pusher to push it over the cab, almost onto the enamel **[M]**. With your finger, confirm the placement, pressing the tab down on the enamel. Repeat with the tab on the opposite side. It's normal for the piece to move a little as the prongs press against it. Hold the enamel cab steady to center it as you push each tab down. Continue pushing the tabs down in pairs of opposites until complete **[N]**.

Secure the tabs

Using the handle of the prong pusher in a rocking motion, gently ease each tab down further to tighten the setting **[O]**.

Form the bail

Using a dowel or the handle of an awl, bend the long stem around the cab to form a bail **[P]**. The end of the tab can be turned up carefully with roundnose pliers to make an S-curve. Add patina if desired.

Spiral Wire Necklace

Learn how to embed playful wire spirals into enamel, and then connect and articulate the enamel shapes in this project.

materials
- 24-gauge copper, ½x⅞" (13x22mm)
- 24-gauge copper, ¹¹⁄₁₆" (18mm) square
- 19-gauge dark annealed steel wire, 18" (46cm)
- 24-gauge dark annealed steel wire, 6–12" (15–31cm)
- 5mm gunmetal jump rings, 10
- chain, 16" (41cm)
- clasp
- size 11 or 15 seed beads
- 1510 Ozone
- 1319 Bitter
- 2850 Sunset Orange

tools & supplies
- basic enameling toolkit
- two-hole metal punch
- indelible markers
- steel bench block
- chainnose pliers
- roundnose pliers
- wire cutters
- goldsmith's hammer

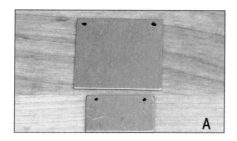

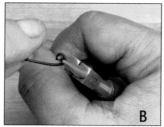

Prepare the metal

Mark holes at the top corners of each of the copper shapes using an indelible marker **[A]**. Punch the holes and save the copper dots for another project. Clean the metal pieces, rinse, and dry.

Counterenamel

Counterenamel the square and the rectangle. Let the pieces cool completely, clean off any firescale, and prepare the metal for enameling the fronts.

Fire base coats

Sift and fire a base coat and second coat, if desired, on both pieces. Allow to cool. I used bitter green on the square and ozone blue on the rectangle.

Make the spirals

Make a large spiral for the square: First, use roundnose pliers to make a small loop on the end of a 3" piece of dark annealed steel wire **[B]**. Hold the loop flat with chainnose pliers in your dominant hand, with the tail of wire in your other hand **[C]**. Roll the loop toward the wire, with the chainnose pliers and your fingers, to form a spiral.

You can make it tight or loose, but leave extra wire at the end to make a loop to connect the spirals to the rectangle. Repeat the steps to make a smaller spiral for the square and three smaller spirals for the rectangle. Use roundnose pliers to make simple loops on the ends of the two spirals that will be embedded on the square. The spirals for the rectangle do not need tails or loops.

Flatten the spirals

Place each spiral on the steel bench block and use a polished goldsmith's hammer to flatten the wire **[D]**. I have not had problems with this damaging my hammer, but to be safe, strike gently. Make sure each spiral will sit flush on the enamel pieces after hammering. If not, flatten them with the rawhide mallet on the steel bench block.

TIP

For the spirals that are embedded in the enamel, I used dark annealed steel wire because I like the contrast of the black on the enamel; 18-gauge copper wire will also work. Don't use plated wire; the plating will burn off.

E

F

G

Place the wires

Before you attach the wire to the enamel, check the placement of the wires, making sure the loops above match up with the holes below **[E]**. If they don't, adjust them with your pliers until they're correct. Mark the enamel with an indelible marker where the loops should rest before the wires are removed for sifting. Make sure the mark is dark enough to see through the sifted enamel in the next step.

Sift a light coat

Sift a light coat with colors of your choice over each piece and place on trivets. Make sure the pieces are level.

Embed the wire

Add the wire spirals on top of the pieces, making sure the loop is off the edge and in the correct place, and the wire sits flush on the enamel. Begin to heat from below. Be prepared with steel tweezers in case the wire needs to be pushed down into the enamel as it goes through its firing stages **[F]**. Repeat for both pieces and allow to cool.

Check the attachment

Check that all the wires are securely embedded in the enamel. The enamel should have risen around the edges of the wire, as if it is hugging them.

Form a double-ended spiral

Create a spiral on both ends of a 3–4" (76–100mm) piece of 19-gauge steel wire to fit above the square shape **[G]**.

Connect the wire to the square

Using 24-gauge steel wire, coil through the hole and around the spiral bar. Wrap around the bar and back through the hole a few times, allowing space between the bar and the square **[H]**. Cut the wire and tuck the end in.

Use chainnose pliers to keep space between the bar and the square as you wrap **[I]**. Add a seed bead every few wraps so you end up with 5–6 beads in the center of the wrapped wire.

Attach the jump rings

Attach the wire loops to the holes in the rectangle with jump rings. If the wires were embedded well into the enamel, the connection will be very strong. But the wires can come loose if you pull too hard while adding the jump rings, so work carefully. If the pieces hang unevenly, use chainnose pliers to carefully adjust the loops or the size of the jump rings.

Finish the necklace

Make three spiral-end connectors from 19-gauge wire, wrap them with 24-gauge wire and seed beads, and connect them to the pendant with varied lengths of chain. Attach half of the clasp to each chain end.

Birds of a Feather

Create your own menagerie of whimsical birds in brilliant and colorful enamels, and use them in jewelry as charms or pendants. You'll draw a design directly onto metal and practice embedding wire in enamel.

materials
- 22-gauge copper sheet, 3" (76mm) square
- 18-gauge copper wire, 3"
- 1870 Orient Red (or other opaque color)
- 1940 Steel

tools & supplies
- basic enameling toolkit
- fine artist paintbrush or pointed clay-shaper
- wire cutters
- chainnose pliers
- steel bench block
- rawhide mallet
- jeweler's saw
- 2/0 saw blades
- French shears
- roundnose pliers
- half-round flat file

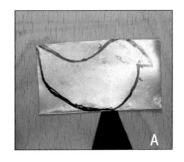 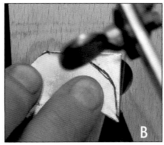 

Create the design

Draw a bird shape on the copper sheet with an indelible marker **[A]**. (You can practice by tracing my birds on the facing page.)

Saw or shear

Use either a jeweler's saw or shears to cut out the shape of the bird **[B]**.

File and sand

File the convex edges with the flat side of the half-round file until they have a smooth finish. Use the half-round side to file the concave curves of the head and tail. Sand both sides with 320-grit wet/dry sandpaper.

Flatten the shape

If the metal isn't flat, place it on the bench block with the concave side down and flatten it with a rawhide mallet.

Punch a hole and clean

Punch a hole for the eye with the screw-down punch. Clean the metal. Before counterenameling, decide which direction you'd like the beak to face.

Counterenamel

Counterenamel the back and allow the piece to cool.

Make the legs and bail

Fold a 3" (76mm) piece of 18-gauge copper wire in half around the tip of the roundnose pliers. The loop should be large enough to fit a jump ring later. Leave the legs straight, but bend the ends up to help balance the wire during enameling. Clean the wire.

Embed the wire

Place the wire on the counterenamel side, and carefully sift on more counterenamel over the wires where they sit on the enamel. Make it a thick coat that completely covers the wires **[C]**. Fire from below until glossy and the wires are embedded. Allow to cool. Clean, rinse, and dry.

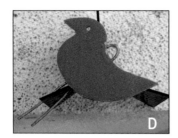

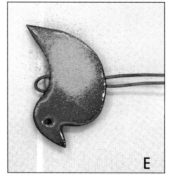

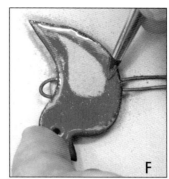

Fire a base coat

Fire one or two coats on the front. Be careful not to fill the eye with enamel. Place the shape on the trivet, with a wire leg on each side of one of the trivet's three supports to hold the wires during firing **[D]**.

Fire on the wing shape

Sift on a small amount of a contrasting color of enamel for the wing **[E]**. Using a fine paintbrush or a clay-shaper, refine the shape by brushing enamel away **[F]**. Clean off any excess enamel and fire again **[G]**.

Bend the feet

Hold the wire firmly with your fingers to keep it steady. Use chainnose pliers to bend ¼" (7mm) of each end at a right angle to make the feet **[H]**.

Serendipity Enameled Bead

This fast project demonstrates how to cut, texture, and shape metal into a tube, and how to roll it in enamel to create a custom bead.

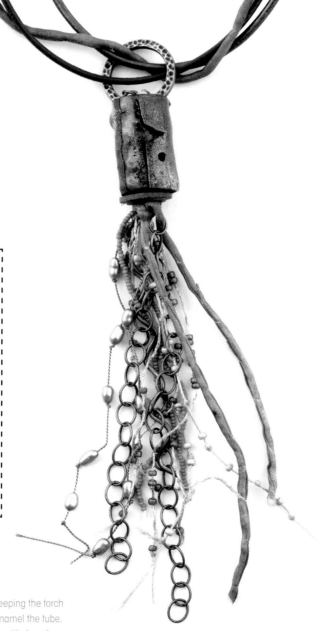

materials
- 24-gauge copper, 1x2" (26x51mm)
- 19-gauge dark annealed steel wire, 8" (20cm)
- 1010 Undercoat (white)
- 2030 Medium Fusing Clear
- mix of transparent and opaque colors

tools & supplies
- basic enameling toolkit
- texture hammers
- screw-down punch
- dimple pliers (1, 3, or 5mm)
- steel bench block

TIP This project requires keeping the torch lit for longer than usual to repeatedly enamel the tube. Start with a full tank and let the butane settle for a few minutes before firing.

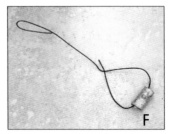

Cut, file, and sand

Cut a 1x1½" (26x38mm) rectangle of 24-gauge copper sheet with shears. A bit of unevenness can add interest, so it doesn't have to be precise. File to remove any sharp edges. Trim a V-shaped notch from one of the short sides **[A]**.

Texture

With dimple pliers, create texture **[B]**. Make some raised to make bumps and others facing the opposite way as dimples. Punch random holes with the screw-down punch for more texture.

Anneal and form the tube

Anneal the copper on the kiln brick, quench, and cool (see the Foldformed Leaf Pendant, p. 66). Wrap the softened metal around a pen or dowel, bringing the two ends together with the notched end slightly overlapping the other end. If the bead needs a little tweaking, use half-round pliers: Place the rounded jaw on the inside of the bead **[C]** and adjust the ends so they fit snugly **[D]**. Pickle for

5–10 minutes. Rinse and dry completely. Use a cotton swab to dry the interior of the bead. The inside of the bead will be left with a patina of firescale after all enameling is finished.

Prepare the enamels

In a ceramic dish, make small piles of different enamels, including undercoat white, clear, and a mix of your favorite transparent and opaque colors **[E]**. Don't use too much since they'll most likely mix and be contaminated. Put the dish on the tile in your firing area so you can safely use the torch and dip the bead into the dish while it's hot.

Set up the bead on wire

Cut 8" (20cm) of dark annealed steel wire and string the bead on it. Leaving a bit of slack so the bead can roll, tie the wire into a loose triangle with a long handle. Twist the ends to secure the triangle while you enamel **[F]**.

G

H

I

J

Dip and fire

Turn on the torch and hold it in your nondominant hand. This technique takes some dexterity, so hold the wire in your dominant hand. Heat the bead with the tip of the blue flame until it glows **[G]** and dip it immediately into the clear fusing flux. Roll it around in the powder, sticking enamel to it, and then heat it again to glossy. Dip again while it's still hot, but try to cover a new part of the bead. Fire the enamel again **[H]**.

Continue dipping into and firing each color, adding white beneath the transparent colors and covering the entire bead. If you run out of fuel during firing, turn off the torch and carefully refuel it. Let it stand for 5–10 minutes, then repeat the process of dipping and firing until you're satisfied with the look. Let the bead cool completely to reveal the colors. If the bead sticks to the wire, tap the edge of the bead against the tile or hold with a towel and gently twist to release it.

Add colors and dots

Now you can add color and embed dots with more control, especially if the colors were a little muddied from dipping. Spray one side of the bead with a holding agent, and sift on an opaque base, such as undercoat white, for transparent colors. Place the bead on a trivet and add dots of transparent enamel with a straw or line sifter. Let the enamel dry for 10 minutes **[I]**.

Fire the bead on trivet

Aim the flame directly into the bead, angling toward the sifted enamel on top **[J]**. Heat until glossy and stop. If the bead sticks to the trivet, tap the trivet against the tile to release it. Let it cool.

TIP

Enjoy embellishing your enameled tube beads. I used handmade headpins, chain, fiber, knotted pearls, and bead caps.

Riveted Hearts Pendant

Riveting connects layers of metal without soldering. This style of rivet is made from a short piece of wire that is hammered on each end to lock the layers in place. As you make this pendant, you'll learn how to rivet without cracking the enamel.

materials
- 24-gauge brass funky heart shape, 1x1½" (26x38mm)
- 24-gauge copper funky heart shape, ⅝x1" (16x26mm)
- 14-gauge copper wire for rivet, ½" (13mm)
- 1715 Clover
- 2760 Mauve
- 2220 Chartreuse

tools & supplies
- basic enameling toolkit
- flex shaft or rotary tool
- high-flex blue polishing wheel
- screw-down punch
- half-round hand file
- steel bench block and pad
- bench pin
- rawhide mallet
- chasing hammer
- goldsmith's hammer

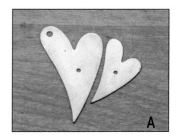

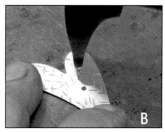

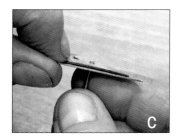

Punch holes in both hearts

It's important to align the holes in the hearts so the rivet can make a good connection. Start with the copper heart. Use the smaller (1/16"/1.5mm) punch to make a hole in the center. Hold the copper heart on top of the brass and make a dot with an ultra-fine-tip indelible marker through the hole onto the brass. Punch a 1/16" hole on that mark through the brass. Punch a third hole with the larger punch near the top of the brass heart for a jump ring **[A]**.

Enamel the copper heart

Clean the copper heart, rinse, and dry. Counterenamel the back and allow to cool. Clean the back, rinse well, and dry. Before you sift, place the heart on the trivet for practice—it's harder to balance than other shapes. Sift on a base coat of pink clover and fire until glossy. Repeat for a more even coat, or add other colors. Allow to cool.

Texture the brass heart

While the enamel heart is cooling, texture the brass heart. I made a random pattern of lines with the sharp wedge of a goldsmith's hammer **[B]**. You can also use the ball end of a chasing hammer or chasing stamps. Texturing and stamping can curl metal, so flatten it by placing the concave side facing the steel bench block and hitting it with the rawhide mallet.

Measure the wire for the rivet

Trim one end of the 14-gauge copper wire flat with flush cutters. Holding the hearts together, pass the wire through the smaller rivet holes. The amount sticking out on each side of the heart sandwich should be the same length as the diameter of the wire (1.6mm) **[C]**. Measure the correct length on one side, turn it over, and mark the other side with a marker **[D]**. Flush-cut the wire, making sure the ends are straight, since it's hard to rivet an angled piece of wire. Using the bench pin as a brace, hold the wire with chainnose pliers and file both ends to a smooth finish **[E]**. Filing spreads the ends a bit, which will help the rivet wire stay in place.

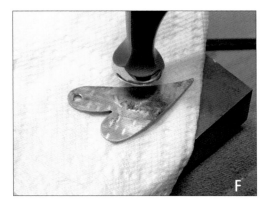

DVD 9 DVD 10

TIP
If you crack the enamel, you can fix it! Wearing a dust mask or respirator, smooth the crack with 320-grit wet/dry sandpaper. Brush on a small amount of Klyr-Fire, sift new enamel over the crack, and brush any excess off the rivet. Place the piece on a trivet and fire until the entire piece is glossy. Allow to cool. Clean the metal again and finish the rivet.

Rivet the hearts together

Place a piece of doubled paper towel or a cloth towel on top of the steel bench block. Put the hearts on the towel with the enamel side facing the steel bench block. Make sure the right amount of wire is above the brass heart. Hammer the wire down very gently with the flat face of the goldsmith's hammer **[F]**. If you widened the rivet enough, it won't fall through the hole when the heart is lifted. It doesn't have to be perfectly smooth; the rivet will be polished later with a power tool.

Flip the hearts over, check the length of wire sticking out of the front, and file it shorter if necessary **[G]**. Place the hearts on top of the towel, enamel side up. Cover half of the heart, including the rivet, with a paper towel to shield the enamel. Press the towel down to see the rivet. Using the ball end of the chasing hammer, gently strike the rivet three times, then check the rivet **[H]**. Repeat if needed to tighten the rivet, although it doesn't have to be flush to the enamel; polishing the rivet will create a burr that brings the rivet closer to the enamel. Make sure to only hit the wire and not the enamel, or it will crack!

Polish and soften the rivet

Place a blue high-flex polishing wheel on a mandrel in your rotary tool or flex shaft. Smooth and round the rivet heads with the wheel **[I]**.

Gingko Leaf Pendant

Saw out a ginkgo leaf from
copper sheet, create a double
bail, and accent it with multiple
layers of enamels.

materials
- 22-gauge copper sheet to
  accommodate the drawing
- 2030 Medium Fusing Clear
- 2115 Mars (brown)
- 2220 Chartreuse
- 2840 Mandarin Orange
- 1319 Bitter
- 2330 Avocado

tools & supplies
- basic enameling toolkit
- rubber cement
- screw-down punch
- 2/0 saw blade
- jeweler's saw
- medium-cut file
- bench pin
- tripod with screen
- small half-round file
- 320-grit wet/dry sandpaper

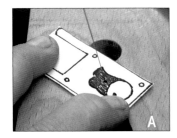

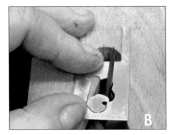

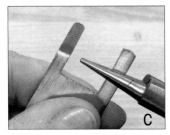

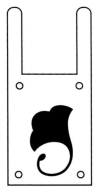

TEMPLATE

Saw out the leaf shape

Create a design on paper or make a copy of the template provided. Cut around the pattern and glue it to the copper with rubber cement. Let it dry for 10 minutes, then punch a hole in the center of the leaf. Load a 2/0 saw blade into the top clamp of the saw frame. Insert the blade through the hole in the copper with the pattern side up, put tension on the blade, and tighten the clamp. Saw out the design. Open the bottom clamp and pull the blade out of the copper. Reload the saw blade in the frame and saw out the outside of the pattern **[A]**.

File and sand the metal

After sawing, refine the shape and edges with a file. Place the piece on a bench pin for support. Use the flat side of a half-round file to file straight and convex edges. Use a small half-round file to clean up the inside of the ginkgo **[B]**.

Sand the front and back with 320-grit wet/dry sandpaper to remove the burrs from filing.

Form the bails

Grasp one tab in the center with round-nose pliers **[C]**. Gently roll the end over to touch the back of the pendant. Repeat for the second tab.

Enamel the pendant

Lightly spray the back with a holding agent. Be sure to cover the rounded tabs. Sift on counterenamel and fire from underneath on a tripod **[D]**. Allow to cool. Clean the metal and sift on a coat of clear as a base coat, fire, and cool. Add a coat of mars brown, fire, and cool. I added a lightly sifted mix of chartreuse, mandarin orange, and a touch of bitter **[E]**. Sift and fire a transparent color over all the layers to add depth to the design.

Cloisonné Lines Pendant

Cloisonné is a great technique for separating enamel colors and creating designs. Learn about washing your enamels, wet-packing techniques, and attaching wires to the enamel.

materials
- 24-gauge copper disk, 1¼" (32mm) diameter
- 18-gauge round copper wire, 5" (13cm)
- 2030 Medium Fusing Clear
- 1319 Bitter
- 1308 Lichen
- 1360 Jungle
- 1150 Woodrow (brown)
- 1335 Pea

tools & supplies
- basic enameling toolkit
- eyedropper
- paper towel
- nylon-jaw flatnose pliers
- assorted fine-tip brushes
- pencil
- paper
- ruler
- screw-down punch
- cloisonné wire cutters or side cutters
- files for enamels or emery board
- wet-packing tool
- fine dental tool or awl
- alundum stone
- glass brush
- high-flex blue polishing wheel

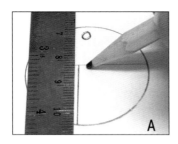 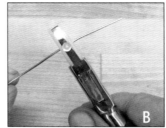 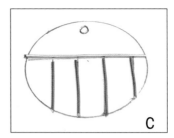

 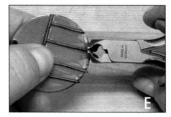 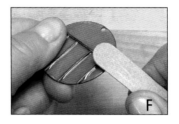

Punch a hole
Punch a hole near the top of the disk for a jump ring.

Sketch the cloisonné design
With a pencil, make several tracings of the disk on a piece of paper so you can experiment with designs.

Draw a pattern of lines to define cells for the cloisonné **[A]**. I recommend straight lines for your first cloisonné piece; they will be the easiest to lay out on the enamel. Use colored pencils or markers to sketch in colors for each cell.

Straighten and cut wires
Grasp a length of wire with the nylon-jaw pliers, just above your fingers, and pull the wire through the jaws to straighten it **[B]**. Following your sketch, cut wire pieces to size with cloisonné wire cutters. Both ends should be flat **[C]**. Clean the disk and the wires. Place the wires on the design so you know where they go.

Counterenamel and clean
Counterenamel the back of the disk using a mix of all the colors you will use on the front. I recommend two coats of counterenamel to help minimize any warping, since there will be multiple coats fired on the front. Clean the metal, rinse, and dry.

Fire the base coat
Fire a base coat of medium fusing clear on the front of the disk and allow to cool.

Add Klyr-Fire
For cloisonné, Klyr-Fire works best as a holding agent to bond the wires to the enamel. Spray or brush a fine coat of Klyr-Fire on the entire front of the disk.

Fire on the wires
Place the disk level on a trivet. With tweezers, position each of the wires for the design and let dry for 15 minutes. Fire from below to glossy. Have bentnose tweezers ready in case the wires need a little help to slump into the enamel **[D]**.

Remove from the trivet and allow to cool on the tile. Cut off any excess wire using cloisonné wire cutters tilted at a slight angle toward the center **[E]**. With an emery board, gently sand the wire until it's smooth and beveled **[F]**.

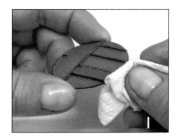

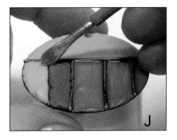

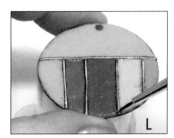

Prepare the enamels

Enamel is best packed into the cells when it is clean and wet. Wash the opaque colors you plan to use. Set up at a clean and level space, with the piece raised on a smaller platform, to make it easier to pick up later.

Have a cup of clean water nearby. If you washed your enamels a while ago, they might be too dry for wet-packing and you'll need to add water with an eyedropper **[G]**. The enamel should be thick enough so it stays on when picked up with the wet-packing tool. Scoop up a small amount of the first enamel color with the wet-packing tool. Drop it in the cell and spread it with the spatula **[H]**. With a wet brush, tamp down the enamel. Notice how it spreads even more to fill the cell. Level the enamel and remove any air bubbles by gently tapping with a file handle or similarly weighty tool on the side of the piece.

Blot

To speed up drying time, it's important to remove excess water. Place a piece of paper towel at the edge of the cell to absorb excess moisture **[I]**.

Fill in all the cells and scrape the wires

Repeat the wet-packing steps until all the cells have been filled and the excess water removed. With the edge of the wet-packing tool, gently scrape the wires to remove any stray grains of glass **[J]**.

Blot again and brush wires clean

Use a paper towel to blot one last time, removing water from all the freshly packed cells **[K]**. With a fine-tip paintbrush, gently follow all the wires and brush them clean **[L]**. It's essential

DIY wet-packing tool

To make your own wet-packing tools with inexpensive copper wire from the hardware store, buy 12" (31cm) of 12-gauge insulated electrical wire (enough to make a few tools). Use wire cutters to strip off 1" (26mm) of insulation. File the end of the exposed wire flat with a hand file. Cut the wire to about 4" (10cm). File the other end flat, but leave the insulation for a comfortable grip. Forge ½" (13mm) of the copper wire into a flat paddle shape with the goldsmith's hammer **[photo]**. File the flattened end to make a tiny spatula.

  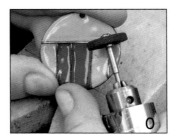

TIP

Rub some Renaissance wax over the surface to protect it and retain the finish on the wires.

to clear stray enamel from the wires if you want a smooth surface with nicely polished wires.

Dry the enamel

Transfer your piece to a safe place and allow it to dry for 1–2 hours. If you fire while the enamel is still wet, the enamel will start jumping out of place **[M]**. If this happens, stop and let the piece cool. Take it back to your wet-packing area and clean it up; it's easier to fix the enamels while they're slightly wet. Wet the paintbrush to add a little water to the cell you're working on. Gently remove any enamel colors that are in the wrong cells and tamp the cells smooth with the brush. Blot again and let it dry—for a bit longer this time.

Fire

Place the piece on the trivet and fire to glossy **[N]**. After the piece has cooled, check the levels of the enamels in the cells. Enamels will sink after firing. Does a cell need one or two more coats of

enamel to reach the level of the wire? If so, repack and fire again.

Stone the enamel

Take the piece to the sink and use an alundum stone to even out the enamel and cloisonné wires. Grind the stone over the surface under running water. Rinse well. Remove any glass dust with the glass brush. Dry it off.

Flash-fire

After stoning, the enamels are matte. To bring back their shiny surface, place the piece on the trivet and fire to the glossy stage. This is called flash-firing.

Polish the wire

After flash-firing, the wires will be black. For a clean look, polish the wires: Pickle the piece for 5 minutes and use a rotary tool or flex shaft with a high-flex blue polishing wheel to smooth the metal without damaging the enamel **[O]**.

Cityscape Pendant

Learn how to use cloisonné wire as you build the cells of this cityscape. This project will take more time, patience, and precision than the Cloisonné Lines Pendant project, but you will be rewarded with a detailed jewelry piece made using what is thought to be the oldest enamel technique.

materials
- 24-gauge copper, 1¼" (32mm) square
- copper cloisonné wire, 1–2 ft. (31–61cm)
- assorted transparent enamels
- 1–3 opaque enamels

tools & supplies
- basic enamel toolkit
- cloisonné wire cutters or side cutters
- fine-tip paintbrush
- fine-tip tweezers
- fine awl or dental tool
- wet-packing tool
- roundnose pliers
- chainnose pliers
- flush cutters
- pen
- paper
- screw-down punch
- nylon-jaw flatnose pliers
- baby food jars or plastic spoons
- cup with distilled water
- eyedropper
- paper towels

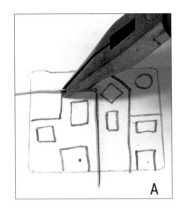

A

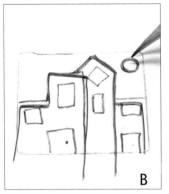

B

C

TIP

Purchased cloisonné wire is dead soft. Many enamelists make their own cloisonné wire with a rolling mill. This hardens the metal, so they anneal and pickle it so it will be more malleable. Annealing also helps prevent it from changing shapes or curving while being fired.

Sketch your design

Draw rough outlines of the metal square and then sketch a few designs for your buildings, doors, and windows. Because cloisonné wire is flat and will be fused on its edge to the base, plan a design with angles—the wire will be easier to position with bends rather than just straight lines.

Straighten the cloisonné wire

Straighten the cloisonné wire with the nylon-jaw pliers to remove any kinks.

Create the design in wire

Cut and bend pieces of wire to match your sketch. Whenever possible, include a bend in each piece of wire **[A]**.

Start with a piece of cloisonné wire that is longer than needed and use chainnose pliers to make sharp bends to match the pattern. Make sure the wires sit flush on the paper after bending. Any extra wire can be trimmed after firing **[B]**. Use chainnose and roundnose pliers to make small shapes like the windows. The ends of these closed shapes should touch to better contain the enamel later.

Punch holes and clean the metal

Punch holes in the corners and clean the metal. Clean the cloisonné wire by pickling it for 10 minutes. Rinse and dry.

Counterenamel, clean, and fire a base coat

Counterenamel the back of the square and clean the front. Fire a base coat of clear on the front and allow to cool.

Fire on the cloisonné wires

Brush on a coat of Klyr-Fire and place the piece on the trivet. With fine-tip tweezers, not your enameling tweezers, arrange all of the small cells you prepared, using your design as a guide. Let it dry for 10 minutes. To fire, heat the kiln brick under the trivet until there is no bubbling, and then heat the trivet. Finally, bring the flame directly under the piece and fire until glossy and you see the wires slump into the enamel **[C]**. You can use bentnose tweezers to ease the wires into the enamel if they need a little help. Allow to cool and check to make sure all the wires are embedded. If they are not completely embedded, sift on a bit of enamel and refire.

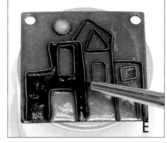

Trim any excess wire

Using cloisonné pliers or a good pair of side cutters, trim all the excess wire around the edges. Cut at a slight inward angle to help prevent sharp points around the edges and make it easier to fill in the enamel flush with the edges later **[D]**.

Wet-packing

If your enamels weren't cleaned earlier, wash them now. Pack the cells with wet enamel (see the Cloisonné Lines Pendant, p. 103) **[E]**. If you have tiny areas to fill, use a pointed steel awl or old dental tool to spread the enamel **[F]**. The enamel should be level and even with the tops of the wires. Use the wet-packing tool to scrape off any excess on the wires.

With transparent enamels, you can create a gradation of colors in the same cell. Start by using lighter tints and adding darker colors on top as you add and fire progressive coats of enamel.

To add silver foil, place it over the clear fusing coat, then fire another coat of clear fusing over it, and then add the wet transparent enamel colors.

Blot and brush

Use a piece of paper towel to blot the entire piece or just sections at a time to reduce water and speed up drying time. Let your piece dry for 1–2 hours **[G]**. Use a fine-tip paintbrush to clean any enamel off the tops of the wires.

Fire

After the piece is semidry but not totally dried out, place it on the trivet and slowly heat it, making sure the enamel doesn't flake or pop. Fire until glossy and allow to cool. Repeat the process of wet-packing, cleaning, drying, and firing until the enamel reaches the same level as the cloisonné wire. Allow to cool.

Stone and brush

After the piece is cool, grind the alundum stone over the surface under running water until the glass is dull and the wires are even with the enamel. Use the glass brush underwater to clean off any glass dust. Rinse well and dry.

Flash-fire and polish

Flash-fire the cloisonné to bring back the glossy surface. Allow it to cool. Polish it as described in the Cloisonné Lines Pendant.

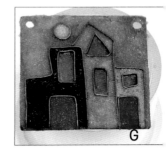

TIP Speed up the drying process by setting the piece under a warm light.

Plique-à-Jour Dots Earrings

Plique-à-jour is a lovely traditional enameling technique. The French term means "letting in daylight." In plique-à-jour, you suspend enamel in cells that have no backing, allowing light to shine through like stained glass. The technique takes a long time to perfect, but this project lets you practice filling open dots on an enameled piece of copper. Watch as the capillary action works its magic, drawing the enamel to fill the small cells and stay in place.

materials
- 18-gauge copper oval with hanging loop, 1⅛ x⅝" (29x16mm)
- pair of earring wires
- Klyr-Fire
- 1208 Cream
- 2850 Sunset Orange
- 2340 Glass
- 2530 Water
- 2240 Olive

tools & supplies
- basic enameling toolkit
- #5/0 sable paintbrush
- dish of water
- 2 trivets
- eyedropper for Klyr-Fire
- eyedropper for water
- 320-grit wet/dry sandpaper
- 200-mesh sifter with pan
- enamel washing supplies
- palette or small plastic containers with lids

Punch holes

Use an indelible marker to mark dots where you want holes to be. Use the screw-down punch to make holes.

Sand and clean

Sand both sides of the metal using 320-grit wet/dry sandpaper **[A]**. Pickle the metal for 2 minutes or use Penny Brite to clean it. Rinse and dry.

Counterenamel

Use black or a combination of colors to counterenamel both pieces.

Clean off firescale

Clean the side that was exposed to the flame.

Fire a base coat

I used cream as a base coat so the transparent dots would show up well.

In the next step, if the colors are not cleaned off from the surface of the cream, they will bleed onto the top, which I happen to like. If you like this look, leave the colors on the surface. If not, wipe them off well with a brush. An option would be to use a darker coat of enamel as the base coat; when you fill the dots, any extra color will not be so obvious on the surface.

Sift and clean enamels

Transparent enamels used for plique-à-jour can be sifted through a 200-mesh screen to remove large particles of enamel for the best clarity. Notice the difference between the enamel in the blue sifter (80-mesh powder that is used for basic sifting) and the fine enamel powder in the red tray **[B]**. Wash the fine powder. Very fine enamel shows the true color, which helps illuminate the design and bring out the effect of miniature stained glass.

Set up washed enamels

Separate the enamel by color in small wells or containers such as a painters palette, plastic spoons, or contact lens containers. If they dry out, you can rehydrate the enamel by adding a few drops of distilled water until you get the proper consistency **[C]**. The enamel should be wet, but when picked up from the dish, the small drops should remain on the brush so it can transfer easily to the cell you want to fill.

TIP Don't worry if you don't have a 200-mesh sifter. For these small dots, it's OK to use washed transparent enamels that haven't been finely sifted. Scoop a small amount of enamel out of the container with the sifter, sift into a plastic spoon, and add a few drops of distilled water. It will work fine, but might not fire to a brilliant color as the finer sifted and washed enamel would. When working with a more open design or a pierced work, use fine mesh to produce purer color.

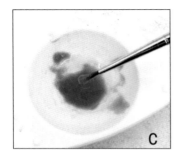

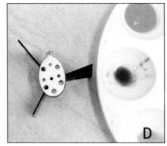

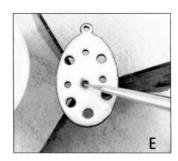

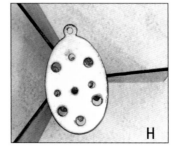

Set up the piece

Place the oval you will work on onto a cold trivet next to the enamels **[D]**.

Add Klyr-Fire

Brush a very small amount of Klyr-Fire on the inside edge of each cell to add some bonding action for the enamel. Too much Klyr-Fire can cause cloudiness. Some enamelists add Klyr-Fire to the enamel itself, which you can try with caution: If you add too much, it can have the opposite effect and the enamel may pull away from the edges instead. Practice and patience are vital as you fill the dots.

Fill the dots

Pick up a dot of the first color with the tip of the brush and place it in the first cell **[E]**. Continue filling more cells with the same color, then rinse the brush and move on to a new color **[F]**. Brush off any excess enamel on the surface if you want. Blot the edges of the piece with a piece of paper towel. Allow to dry for 30 minutes or more until the enamel looks like powder again.

Fire

After all the holes are filled and the surface is satisfactory, use your fingers to transfer the piece to a trivet on the kiln brick. Turn on the torch and aim the flame at the kiln brick so it is slightly raised and points down into the corner of the trivet. This will ensure that the heat radiates upward to the piece. Don't heat from underneath at this point. Fire until it reaches the sugar-coat stage, which will be very quick **[G]**. If it goes beyond that stage on the first firing, the enamel will pull away from the edges of the cell **[H]** and it will take more time to fill all the cells and fire the piece completely.

TIP
File the tips of the trivet to soften them so you don't poke yourself while filling the cells.

TIP On the first firing, take the enamel to sugar coat; on the second, to orange peel; and on the third or fourth, take the enamel to the final stage. After the first firing, the enamel will have sunk and shrunk. The second will have some shrinkage as well, but much less. Fill the enamel so it is level with the surface of either the metal or any previous enamel coat on the piece.

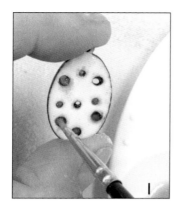

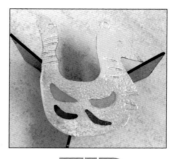

TIP

Shapes with sharp angles are more difficult to fill. Even cells with a slight curve are easier. When filling cells that are not dots, place a bit of enamel on one end and drag the enamel across the cell with the brush to fill the entire space.

Fill again

If you fire to the sugar-coat stage, all the enamel will stay intact but will shrink slightly, so you can add just a small amount of enamel to fill each cell to the level of the enamel base coat. If the enamel has pulled away from the sides, you will need to fill them all with small amounts of enamel **[I]**.

Fire again

If the first firing was successful to the sugar-coat stage, then this firing should be taken to the orange-peel stage. If the enamel pulled away and you had to fill up the entire cell, then count this as a first firing and take it to the sugar-coat stage. Allow to cool. Fill again if needed.

Fire the final stage

When you have gone through the first and second firings and all the cells are filled and the piece is satisfactory, fire again and this time take the piece to the final stage so all the cells glow **[J]**. Turn the torch off and allow the piece to cool.

Repeat the filling and firing steps for the remaining oval. Add earring wires to finish the earrings.

plique-à-jour pointers

1. If you are using the same trivet for filling and firing, you can always quench and dry it once the piece is removed and placed on the tile to cool. That will ensure you will not burn yourself when you need to use the trivet for the next step.

2. If you are filling cells and leaving a bare metal surface around them, you will need to sand the piece with wet/dry sandpaper under running water, starting with coarse 220-grit and moving up to 600-grit. Then the piece can be stoned. The enamel will be matte at this point, so you can either leave it or flash-fire the entire piece.

3. Firing to final stage too quickly can cause the enamel to slump to the back of the piece and form a huge lump.

4. Sometimes mica is used as a backing when filling and firing. You can experiment with this, but be aware that mica can stick to the enamel or the metal and requires a lot of cleaning.

5. When using fine-silver pierced metal, some artists will use a titanium backing while filling.

6. When piercing metal to use with plique-à-jour, 18-gauge or 20-gauge will work best.

7. If your enamel is not firing and filling the cells, you can add a drop of Klyr-Fire to the enamel itself to help it bond. Don't add too much; this can cause cloudiness. You can always add more water as the enamel dries.

Soldered Reversible Pendant

Being able to enamel on soldered metal opens the door to lots of possibilities for jewelry designs. This piece introduces the basics of soldering metal and enameling the resulting piece to make a reversible pendant of open circles.

materials
- 18-gauge washers, 1 ea. of 3 assorted sizes (mine were ⅝", ½", and ⁵⁄₁₆"/16, 13, and 8mm ID)
- 8mm gunmetal jump ring
- gunmetal key charm
- eutectic silver solder, ¾"/19mm piece
- 1010 Undercoat (white)
- 2240 Olive
- 2430 Beryl
- 2610 Sky

tools & supplies
- basic enameling toolkit
- basic soldering toolkit
- tripod and screen
- small fine-tip paintbrush
- small straw or line sifter
- 180-grit wet/dry sandpaper

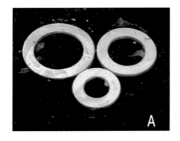

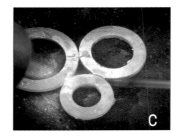

Clean the metal

Metal needs to be clean and degreased before soldering to allow the flux to bond to the surface. Pickle all the washers or clean them with Penny Brite, rinse well, and dry.

Set up for soldering

Eutectic silver solder requires a lot of heat to flow, so it's best done on charcoal, which boosts the heat. Place the charcoal block on the solder board. Paint all the surfaces of the washers with flux. Arrange them on the charcoal so they are touching for soldering **[A]**. Cut three 2mm pieces of eutectic solder, put them on the solder board, and dab a little flux on each one.

Solder the pieces together

Heat the copper pieces gently. When the flux turns clear and glassy, turn off the torch. Place the chip of solder on each join **[B]**. Turn the torch on again and slowly heat all the copper washers together. Use a pick to return any solder that moves out of place.

As the copper starts to glow red, aim the flame at one join at a time. When the solder flows as the metal turns a bright red, have the pick ready to help the solder flow into the join, if necessary **[C]**. Turn off the torch, quench the metal, and pickle for 10 minutes. Rinse and dry well. Make sure the solder flowed into each join. If you need to solder again, repeat the steps to clean, flux, add solder, and heat again.

TIP If the metal is stuck on the charcoal after soldering, it's because the flux has hardened. Drip a little water on the metal to shock the flux loose. If that doesn't work, warm it with the torch as you nudge it with tweezers until the flux loosens. If you pry it off, you'll take off chunks of charcoal too. Quench, pickle, rinse, and dry.

firing from above

An amazing thing about torch-firing and transparent enamels is that some of the colors go through beautiful changes when you fire from above with the flame directly on the enamel. After you have fired from below and the enamel goes to the orange-peel stage, try bringing the torch to the top and watch the oxides come to the surface, creating lovely metallic colors as the enamel turns glossy. Don't overfire or you can burn the enamel.

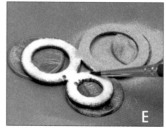

TIPS

Sand the solder

Using 180-grit wet/dry sandpaper, sand the metal on all sides after soldering to remove firescale and excess solder. Too much solder can keep the enamel from fusing to the metal, and excess solder under transparent enamels can blacken during firing and muddy the color. Be thorough and remove all of it before enameling.

Clean and sift on counterenamel

Clean and dry the metal for enameling. Sift an even coat of counterenamel on the back. I made a custom mix of several blues, so the pendant is just as pretty on the back as the front.

Set up for enameling

Place two trivets on a mesh screen on a tripod, and place the piece on top. Make sure all the rings are evenly supported [D]. Using two trivets helps keep the piece from sagging even if the solder reflows a little during enameling.

Fire to glossy

Fire the pendant from below, heating the entire piece evenly [D]. Then concentrate the flame on each ring, taking each one in turn to the final glossy stage. Let the piece cool on the tile. Pickle for 5 minutes, rinse, and dry.

Fire on top coats

Sift on a base coat of undercoat white, set up for enameling on two trivets again, and fire. Allow the piece to cool. Sift a different transparent enamel color on each ring and brush off any excess, especially where the rings are joined [E]. A line sifter or small straw will dispense small amounts of enamel near the joins to prevent any overspill. Fire with the same trivet setup. Melting in glass seed beads or stringers is a finishing option. Attach the key charm to one washer with a jump ring.

Enameled Cabochon Ring

Imagine making custom cabochons: mix colors and layers to make beautiful, stone-like surfaces, or stencil or stamp a design. This project shows you how to bezel-set an enameled cab in a stunning ring.

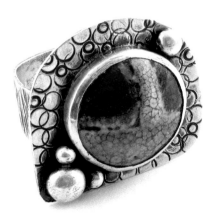

materials
- 20- or 22-gauge sterling sheet, 1½" (38mm) square
- 20-gauge fine-silver wire (or scrap fine silver), 3–4" (76–100mm)
- ³⁄₁₆"-(5mm) wide fine-silver bezel wire (length to fit cabochon)
- ¾"-(19mm) wide 20-gauge sterling sheet for shank, 3" (76mm)
- enameled cabochon

tools & supplies
- basic enameling toolkit
- soldering toolkit
- sterling wire solder: 1" (26mm) each of easy, medium, and hard
- scrap plastic lid
- steel bench block
- rawhide hammer
- chasing hammer or 1 lb. brass hammer
- square or round ring mandrel
- curved burnisher
- goldsmith's hammer
- ruler with millimeters
- polishing tools
- ring clamp
- large multisize forming pliers
- half-round pliers
- dental floss
- Silver Black patina
- 0- or 2-cut half-round hand file
- V-slot bench pin with clamp
- cotton swab
- polishing pad

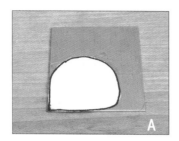

Sketch the base for the setting

For the enameled cabochon, I dapped a 1" (26mm) 24-gauge copper disk and enameled it with multiple layers of color to resemble a stone. Trace around the cab on a piece of paper as a template for your sketch and create a pattern for the base of the setting.

Saw out the base

Cut out the pattern and glue it to 20-gauge sterling silver sheet with rubber cement. Let it dry for 10 minutes [A]. Using a 2/0 saw blade, saw around the pattern.

File, shape, and sand

Hold the base with a ring clamp [B] or near the edge of a bench pin, and file to refine the shape of the piece. Remove the paper pattern and sand both sides with 400-grit wet/dry sandpaper to remove any burrs from filing. Continue sanding to remove any scratches, then use 600-grit to create a satin finish.

Add texture

Place the enameled piece on the base and trace a line around it with a marker [C]. Add texture outside of the mark. This will leave a smooth, level area for the bezel in the center. I used nail sets from the hardware store to stamp a pattern of circles.

Form the bezel

Cut the end of the bezel wire at a right angle to make it easier to make the join later. Use good shears or cutters that won't leave a bevel. Wrap the bezel around the enameled piece, being careful not to crush the soft silver. Keep the bezel straight, and don't let it twist or narrow into a cone. Mark the point where the tail overlaps the start of the bezel [D]. Cut it carefully at a right angle again, flush and without a bevel.

Wrap the bezel around the cabochon again to check the fit. If the ends overlap, trim the wire again. The bezel should be snug against the cab on all sides, and the join should touch or have a gap no larger than 1mm. Close the join for soldering with half-round pliers. With the half-round jaw on the inside, gently bend the ends toward each other until they're parallel. Overlap the ends of the

join, over and under, to create tension until it stays closed. The join should be flush from end to end: If you hold it up to a light, you should see no light shining through the seam. Use a flat needle file to carefully adjust the join if it's out of alignment. Don't twist the bezel; it must lay flat for soldering to the base. After it's closed, pickle for 10 minutes to clean. Rinse and dry.

Solder the bezel

The bezel wire contains no copper to form firescale, so only the join needs to be fluxed. Place the bezel on the charcoal block and make sure the join is still closed. Flux the join, inside and out. Flatten ½" (13mm) of hard solder on the steel bench block with a steel hammer. Cut a 1mm chip of solder and place it on a flat spot on the charcoal block. Pick up the bezel and place the join on the solder. Gently heat the entire bezel until the flux turns clear. Move the heat to the join line and hold until the solder flows up to the top. Quench, pickle, and rinse.

Check the bezel

Reshape the bezel on a ring mandrel, hitting it gently with a rawhide mallet. Check the fit with the cab. Inserting the cabochon into the bezel a few times can stretch it to size if necessary. It should fit easily and completely into the bezel without force, with the bezel flat to the table, and without distorting the sides.

Melt fine-silver balls

Cut three ⅜" (10mm) pieces of 20-gauge fine-silver wire, and a 1" (26mm) piece. Space them out on the charcoal block. Heat each one separately into a shiny silver ball **[E]**. The bottoms will be flat. Pickle for 5 minutes and rinse.

Solder the bezel to the base

If the bottom of the bezel doesn't rest flat against a steel bench block, sand it over a flat surface on a piece of 320-grit sandpaper. Check the fit of the bezel against the base. If there are gaps, flatten the base with a rawhide mallet. If it's still not flat, anneal it: Mark the base with indelible marker, and flux both sides. Heat it on the charcoal until the flux turns clear, the marker fades, and the silver glows a faint red in dim light. Pickle for 10 minutes. The dead-soft metal should flatten easily. Check the fit of the cab in the bezel again.

Use the tripod for soldering so you can heat the thick base from underneath. Heating from above, directly on the bezel, can melt it or make the solder flow all over the fine silver. Use a mesh screen dedicated to soldering (not your enameling screen). Flux both sides of the base and place it on the screen with the bezel on top. Space 2mm chips of medium solder every ¼" (6mm) along the inside of the bezel **[F]**. Heat

TIP
You can leave the base plain, but textured metal is easier to polish.

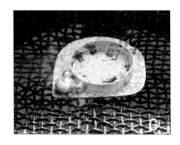

Ring size	Ring blank length (for 20-gauge)
6	54.0mm
6.5	55.3mm
7	56.5mm
7.5	57.8mm
8	59.1mm
8.5	60.3mm
9	61.6mm
9.5	62.8mm
10	64.1mm
10.5	65.3mm

from underneath, slowly at first with a low flame, to let the flux slowly dry out without disturbing the solder. If the solder pallions start to jump around, keep heating until the flux starts to turn clear, and then move the solder back into place with the pick. Increase the flame and move in closer, with the tip of the blue cone just under the base. Move the heat slowly under the base until the solder flows around the seam.

Turn off the torch and place the fine-silver balls on the base with a 1mm chip of medium solder under each one. (You can flatten the solder first.) Heat from underneath until the solder flows and the balls drop to the base **[G]**. Quench, pickle for 15 minutes, rinse, and dry.

Check the cabochon in the bezel with dental floss

Check the fit of the cabochon in the bezel, putting some dental floss underneath it so it doesn't get stuck: Double the floss, place it over the bezel, and put the cabochon inside **[H]**.

Make a ring blank

Cut a strip of 20-gauge sterling for the ring shank. The width of the sample ring is ¾" (19mm). Set dividers to that measurement, and with one leg tracing the straight edge of the sheet, scribe a parallel line **[I]**.

To find the length, measure your ring size with finger gauges or measure a ring that fits with a ring mandrel that is marked with sizes. Use the table on the left to find the length for your ring blank (given in millimeters for accuracy). Mark the length on the sheet metal. Cut out the blank with metal shears.

Flatten the strip with a rawhide mallet and texture it on a steel bench block with the wedge of a goldsmith's hammer to create a texture of lines **[J]**. If the metal starts to curve during hammering, hammer along the edge it's curving toward to straighten it. Hammering stretches the metal, so measure it again and trim to size. Each end of the blank should be a right angle to the length.

enlarging the bezel

If the bezel is slightly too small, it is possible to stretch it after soldering. Put it on a steel ring mandrel and gently hit it all around with a rawhide mallet to remove any wrinkles that might be interfering with the fit. Check it against the enameled piece again. If it's still too small, put it back on the mandrel and strike it with the flat face of a polished goldsmith's hammer. Start by planishing the join and a few millimeters to either side. Check the fit again and repeat, always planishing on fresh metal, until it fits.

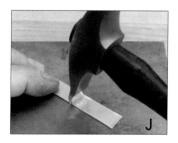

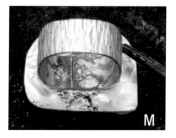

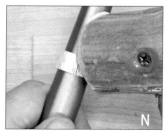

File and form the ring

Texturing can change the edges, so file them to make them straight. To form it into a ring, place one end of the blank inside the jaws of the multisize forming pliers. Turn the pliers to curl the strip halfway **[K]**. Repeat on the other end, curling the ends toward each other.

Close the shank for soldering

With half-round pliers **[L]**, close the ring as you did the bezel for soldering. This will distort the round shape, which is fine, since you can reshape it after soldering. Pickle for 10 minutes, rinse, and dry.

Solder the shank

Cut a 2mm chip from a flattened piece of hard solder. Flux the ring, inside and out, and set the join on the solder chip on the charcoal block **[M]**. Heat the entire ring until the flux turns clear. Move the flame to the join and hold it steady until the solder flows. If it doesn't flow all the way to the top, flip the ring over and add a smaller flat chip of solder. Repeat heating to melt the solder again. Quench, pickle, rinse, and dry.

Solder the setting to the shank

Place the shank on a ring mandrel and hammer it with a rawhide mallet until it's round **[N]**. (I used a rounded square mandrel to make a cushion-shaped ring, so I couldn't confirm the size on a mandrel.) Check the fit on your finger or a mandrel. The line for your size should be in the center of the band. If it's too small, stretch it on the mandrel by texturing it more. Check the size often.

Make a flat spot on the ring for a better join to the base; I recommend filing the join line to hide it under the base. Brace the ring against the bench pin and use the flat side of a hand file to smooth the spot. Check the fit. The base should balance easily on the ring.

Pickle the base and ring for 10 minutes, rinse, and dry. Center the ring on the back of the base and mark its position with an indelible marker. Flux all sides of the base and ring. Cut four 2mm pieces of easy solder and flux them on the solder board. Place the ring base upside down on the charcoal and center the ring on it, using the lines for reference. A

O

P

TIP

Don't worry if the bezel is too high, since that can be fixed during setting. But if the cab doesn't fit in the bezel, you must fix it: Either the bezel will have to be unsoldered and adjusted or you can make a new cab to fit it.

third hand can rest against the shank to help keep it in place. Place two chips of solder on either side of the ring where it touches the base. Heat both the base and ring evenly until all of the flux turns clear **[O]**. As it turns clear, focus the heat on either side of the join and inside the ring until the solder flows. Quench, pickle, rinse, and dry.

Check the bezel height

Place dental floss across the bezel and under the cab, and check the fit again. If the bezel is much higher than the point where the cab tapers, adding padding underneath it can raise it up. It also makes the cab look much bigger!

Use plastic from yogurt or cottage cheese container lids to raise the cab if necessary: Trace around the cabochon and cut along the inside of the line to make some matching disks. I used four layers of plastic for my ring **[P]**. As you add each layer, check the fit until the bezel is only 1–2mm above the taper of the enamel **[figure]**. Don't forget to use that dental floss!

FIGURE

Q

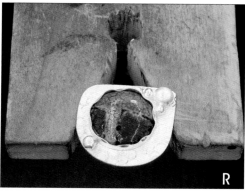

R

Set the cabochon

Remove the floss and push the cabochon into place. Hold the ring in a ring clamp, if you can, with the base resting on the flat jaws. Brace it against the bench pin for support. If the ring won't fit in a ring clamp, use your fingers. Use some scrap leather under the metal where it rests to prevent scratches.

Hold the cab in place with your nondominant hand. Use a curved steel burnisher with the point curved away from the bezel to crimp the bezel down against the cabochon **[Q]**. Push just the part of the bezel that is above the stone, not the whole side. Go to the opposite side and repeat the motion. For example, start at 12 o'clock, then move to 6 o'clock, followed by 9 o'clock and 3 o'clock. Always crimp the bezel in pairs of opposites to avoid making a wrinkle that is difficult to set **[R]**. Continue pushing down the bezel until it is completely set against the enamel.

Now turn the burnisher over and raise the ring, resting the edge of the base on the leather. Hold the burnisher like a potato peeler and bring the burnisher

toward you, rubbing back and forth with pressure along the edge of the bezel. This will polish the bezel and remove any fine gaps. Try not to hit the enamel. Some enamel surfaces can take it, but it's not worth taking any chances.

Polish the ring

Polish the ring with a flex shaft or rotary tool. I recommend polishing inside the ring with split mandrels and 320-grit sandpaper, followed by 600-grit. Polish the rest of the ring with radial bristle disks, which won't damage the texture. Move through all five recommended grits for a brilliant shine.

Add patina

I prefer using Silver Black to liver of sulfur as a patina for this ring, because it can be brushed only where I want it. Wear gloves, and apply the patina with a paintbrush or cotton swab. When finished, dip the ring in water mixed with baking soda to neutralize it. Rinse and dry. Rub with a polishing pad to bring back the highlights.

Frilly Flower Ring

This lovely silver ring with a colorful flower challenges you
to enamel on a piece that contains solder with a lower
melting temperature than eutectic solder. It's also an
opportunity to experience how enameling over brilliant
fine silver enhances transparent enamels.

materials
- 22- or 24-gauge fine-silver disk, ¾" (19mm) diameter
- 20-gauge fine-silver wire, ½" (13mm)
- 14-gauge half-round sterling silver wire, 3" (76mm)
- hard silver solder
- 2020 Clear for Silver
- 2340 Glass

tools & supplies
- basic enameling toolkit
- soldering toolkit
- Blazer butane torch
- yellow ochre gouache paint
- paintbrush
- mini burnisher
- third hand
- large multisize forming pliers
- nylon-jaw pliers
- French shears
- ring mandrel
- dapping block
- 220-grit wet/dry sandpaper
- 400-grit wet/dry sandpaper

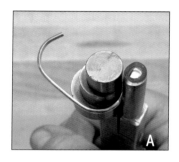

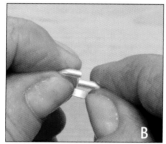

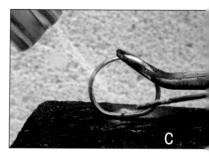

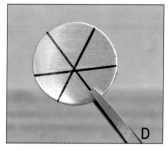

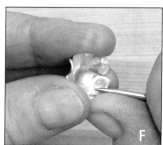

Make a ring blank

Using the chart on p. 120, find your ring size and cut the 14-gauge half-round sterling wire to the corresponding length (the wire is the same thickness as 20-gauge sheet). Make a blank with flat, right-angle ends.

Form and close the ring

Use large multisize forming pliers **[A]** and half-round pliers to form a ring and close the join for soldering. When the ends of the join are parallel, close the ring with tension. Open the ring side-ways and overlap the ends, first on one side, then the other, until the ends snap together and are centered **[B]**. Pickle for 10 minutes, rinse, and dry.

Solder the ring

Flux the ring completely and place it in a third hand with the join on the charcoal block **[C]**. Flatten some hard solder wire and cut a 1mm chip. Heat the entire band until the flux goes glassy, and then apply the solder to the inside of the join.

Reheat the ring, and as it starts to glow a light red, aim the flame directly at the join until the solder flows. Quench, pickle, rinse, and dry. Reshape the ring on the mandrel and check the size. If the ring is too small, use the rawhide mallet to tap it down the mandrel to stretch it up to a half-size larger without adding texture.

Draw lines for the flower

With a marker and a ruler, draw lines on the fine-silver disk, creating six separate sections that will become the petals. Uneven sections are fine **[D]**.

Cut, file, and form the petals

With French shears, cut a small V shape out of each line. Use a triangular needle file to fix the notches and a half-round needle file to round the petals. With 220-grit wet/dry sandpaper followed by 400-grit, sand between each petal **[E]** and the front and back of the disk. Dap the disk into a dome. With a small needle burnisher, go around the edge of each petal until the petals shine **[F]**.

Use your fingers or nylon-jaw pliers to bend the petals for a more natural look.

File the ring and flower

With a half-round hand file, make a flat spot on the bottom of the flower. Brace the flower upside down on the bench pin. Hold the ring in the ring clamp, and file a flat spot at the join. This will make a better join for soldering them together. Pickle for 10 minutes, rinse, and dry.

Solder

Flux the entire sterling ring and the bottom of the fine-silver flower (only the sterling will get firescale and needs flux for protection). Place the flower, petals down, on the charcoal. Hold the band in the third hand and adjust it so the two flat spots are flush and the ring is centered on the flower. Place a 1mm chip of hard solder on either side of the join. Warm both pieces until the flux turns clear, then focus on the join until the solder flows [G]. Quench, pickle for 10 minutes, rinse, and dry.

Protect the join for enameling

The heat of enameling could easily melt the solder again and cause the ring to fall apart, but we can protect the join by getting it dirty (violating the first rule of soldering, "keep it clean"). Yellow ochre gouache paint is a simple and effective anti-flux. Brush a small amount on the join [H]. You don't have to let it dry before enameling.

Sift on a coat of clear fusing

Spray or brush just the interior of the flower with a holding agent, since it is curved and the enamel would slump. Sift 2020 Clear for Silver into the flower, angling the sifter to get full coverage [I]. 2020 is made for fine silver, and a layer of clear will keep the colors true. Let it dry for 10 minutes.

 J

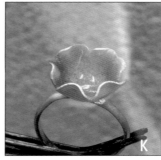 K

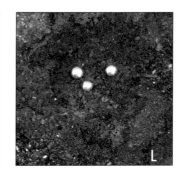 L

Set up to enamel

The ring is difficult to balance in a trivet, and the torch will have to access the flower from all sides during firing. Use a third hand to hold the shank, raised on the tripod above the tile, so it extends **[J]**. Notice how a few kiln bricks create a protective screen behind the third hand.

Fire

Flux just the sterling band to protect it from firescale during firing. If you get yellow ochre on the brush, clean it thoroughly; don't contaminate the flux in the jar. Using a Blazer torch full of fuel and a maximum flame, heat from afar at first, moving the flame closer until the blue tip touches the exterior of the flower. Heat the flower evenly until the enamel goes through its stages to glossy **[K]**. Allow to cool on the third hand.

Fire on a coat of color

Fire on a coat of transparent color. Reapply any yellow ochre or flux, if necessary. Allow to cool.

Embed a fine-silver ball

Cut ½–1" (13–26mm) of 20-gauge fine-silver wire. Place it on the charcoal and melt it into a ball **[L]**. Pickle it for 5 minutes. Sift a second layer of your enamel color over a coat of holding agent. Drop the ball in the center of the flower with tweezers, placing the flat side

 M

down. Let it dry. As you fire and take the enamel to the final stage, the ball will sink into the enamel. Pickle for 5 minutes, rinse, and dry.

Polish and add patina

Use a black silicone polishing wheel to clean up any extra solder where the band is joined to the flower, or on the join of the ring itself. Remove the seam line on the inside of the ring with the same wheel **[M]**. Use radial bristle disks from coarse to fine to polish the ring. Add patina to the base where it touches the ring for an accent of shadow, or leave the entire ring bright, beautiful silver.

Giverny Pendant

Stones set in enamel, a tube bail, and embedded leaves are all part of this pretty project. Thinking of the surface as a painter's canvas will open up a whole garden of possibilities for what you can create with enamels.

materials
- 24-gauge copper sheet, 1x¾" (26x19mm) and 1" (26mm) square
- round copper tubing, ⁵⁄₃₂" (4mm) diameter, 2" (51mm)
- 4mm fine-silver cup bezel
- 4mm garnet
- fine silver dot
- 2030 Medium Fusing Clear
- 1319 Bitter
- 1760 Iris
- 1810 Buttercup
- 2850 Sunset Orange
- 1010 Undercoat (white)

tools & supplies
- basic enameling toolkit
- jeweler's saw
- 2/0 saw blade
- indelible marker
- bench pin
- curved burnisher
- leather scrap

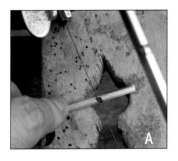

Cut the tubing

Mark the tubing with the length you want for a bail. Load the saw frame with a 2/0 blade. Rest the tubing on the bench pin for support. Angling the blade across the tubing, saw away from you to file a groove on the mark. If the blade catches inside the tubing, continue sawing with forward strokes only, using the smooth direction of the blade **[A]**. Make sure you have something underneath like a drawer to catch the tubing, or else it may fly off into the unknown!

Check the stone in the bezel

Place a piece of dental floss across the bezel, extending over the sides. Put the stone on top of it, and check the fit. Pull up on the floss to pop out the stone.

Clean and counterenamel

Clean the copper rectangle with 320-grit sandpaper. Don't get the tube wet, because water can get trapped inside. Counterenamel the copper rectangle only. I used a mix of different blues. Allow to cool.

Embed the tube

Spray the tube bail with a holding agent and place it on the counter-enamel. Sift more counterenamel over the entire rectangle, sifting a thicker coat around and over the tube **[B]**. Let it dry for 10 minutes. Place a trivet on the kiln brick and fire from below. The enamel should be completely fused all around the bail **[C]**. Clean the front.

Fire on a base coat and colors

Have fun applying colors! Use the small sifter to dust on touches of orange, white, yellow, green, and purple. Fire again. Add more bits of color with the line sifter. Watch how the colors take on depth and vibrancy, and the piece develops more complexity.

TIP

Consider buying a special tool called a tube-cutting jig if you cut a lot of tubing. Sawing tubing on a bench pin is a good alternative.

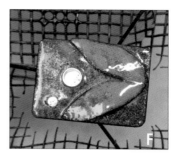

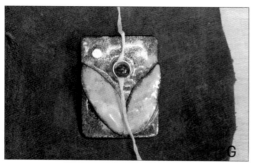

TIP Even calibrated-size stones aren't always exact. Check different stones from the same lot for the best fit.

Cut leaves

Draw the leaf designs on the remaining copper sheet and cut them out with shears. File and sand until you are satisfied with the shapes and smoothness.

Bend the leaves

Create dimension by placing the center of the leaf over a pen and slightly bending it, and then bend the ends of the leaves so they are flush with the enamel piece **[D]**. The leaves don't have to make full contact with the enamel surface; just be sure they touch on the top and the bottom.

Embed the bezel and leaves

Sift a fine coat of clear over the entire piece, then place the bezel, leaves, and fine-silver dot where you want them. Sift bitter green over the leaves **[E]**.

This project can be fired on the kiln brick or tripod **[F]**. Fire until you see the enamel come up and envelop the sides of the bezel as the entire piece turns glossy orange. Do not overfire; this could melt the bezel. Allow to cool. Make sure the leaves are fully embedded (if not, add more enamel and refire). Sprinkle a bit more color and fire for the last time. Allow to cool.

Set the stone

Make sure the stone still fits the bezel: place the piece on a scrap of leather to protect the enamel, and use dental floss as you test the fit **[G]**. Remove the dental floss and push the stone into the bezel. Place the burnisher on one side of the bezel and push in at that point to crimp the metal around the stone **[H]**.

Move to the opposite side of the bezel and repeat the crimping process. Thinking of the piece as a clock, move to noon, 6 o'clock, and so forth, always crimping one side and then its opposite. Go around the bezel carefully, smoothing the metal **[I]**.

Turn the burnisher over and go around the bezel once more to create a tight and even bezel **[J]**.

TIP Another setting option is to use a prong pusher to crimp the sides into the stone. Smooth the bezel with the burnisher.

Amphora Pendant

Vases and vessels have always been part of my jewelry designs. Being able to forge and form dimension in metal is extremely satisfying. And did you know it's possible to make an enameled connection between two pieces of enameled copper? I'll teach you how to do it.

materials
- 24-gauge copper sheet, 3" (76mm) square
- 19-gauge dark annealed steel wire or 18-gauge copper wire, 6" (15cm)
- Klyr-Fire
- 1010 Undercoat (white)
- 2430 Beryl
- 2115 Mars (brown)
- 2220 Chartreuse
- 2030 Medium Fusing Clear

tools & supplies
- basic enameling toolkit
- fine-tip paintbrush
- rubber cement
- tripod with screen
- U-channel hardwood block
- ball-peen hammer

A

B

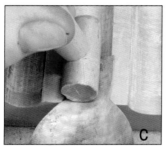

C

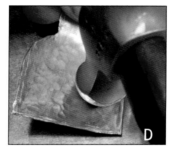

D

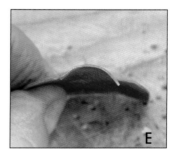

E

Cut the metal

Draw a pattern for the vase directly on the metal and saw or cut out the shape. Sawing will produce cleaner lines and require less cleanup, but it is possible to cut out the shape with metal shears **[A]**. Use the shears to cut a rectangle from the remaining copper so the vase can be centered on it with at least ¼" (7mm) space between it and the edge.

Clean up the edges

File all the edges and sand both sides of each piece of metal **[B]**.

Form the neck

A U-channel hardwood block, also known as a swage, is the perfect tool for forming the neck of the vase **[C]**.

Place the neck in one of the depressions, making sure it is not too tight, and tap it down with the punch until the shape is defined.

TIP
You may find U-channel forming blocks, or swages, in steel as well as hardwood. Some swages come with their own set of punches, short cylinders on handles. You can also use the cylindrical handles of dapping punches. Tap the punches with a rawhide, nylon, or brass mallet.

Form the base of the vase

With a ball-peen hammer, forge the sides of the vessel **[D]**, making the curve of the bottom and the curve of the neck in the same plane **[E]**. As you hammer, the metal will curve **[F]**.

Shape the edges

With the domed side up, position each side of the vase on the edge of the steel bench block and hammer the sides down so they are flush with the steel bench block **[G]**. Use the ball of a ball-peen hammer to work the edges.

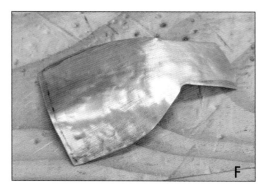

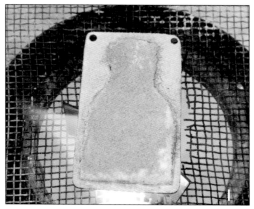

TIP
Using a scrap of wood instead of a steel bench block allows the metal to sink, creating a more domed shape. Another option is to use a wooden dapping block; it is shallow and will not disturb the neck. If the metal is too hard, anneal it and continue shaping. Make several small strikes with the hammer so the edges roll up as you move around, creating a slightly domed piece.

Prepare the base
Make holes in the two top corners of the base, and round all four corners by filing. Sand the front, back, and edges of the rectangle. Pickle both pieces, rinse, and dry well. Counterenamel the base only.

Fire the vase
While the base is in the pickle, spray the top of the vase with a holding agent and sift on a coat of white, fire, and pickle.

Connect the pieces
Remove the base from the pickle, rinse, and dry. Sift on a coat of white, fire, and allow to cool. Place the vase on the base and make sure it is level [H]. Remove the vase, sift a coat of brown on the top of the base, place the vase on top, and fire the two pieces together [I]. Allow to cool. Check if the vase embedded into the enamel of the base.

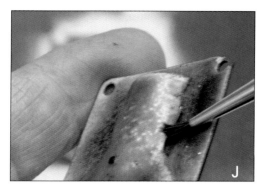

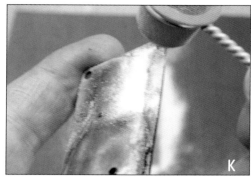

If the vase did not embed in the base enamel, sand the areas where the two pieces touch to clean the surface and make a better join. Rinse off any residue from the paper, and brush a light coat of Klyr-Fire around the edge of the vase where it meets the base **[J]**. With a line sifter, add a coat of 2030 Medium Fusing Clear **[K]**, let it dry 15–25 minutes, and fire. This should connect the two pieces.

TIP
If this technique of joining the pieces with enamel does not work for you, start over and join the pieces with soldering. Use eutectic solder, pickle, and then enamel.

Add enamel

After firing and connecting the two pieces, spray and sift another coat on top of the vase, brush off any excess on the base color, and add some copper dots, if desired **[L]**.

finishing finesse

Experiment with these finishing options on your Amphora Pendant or any other enameling project.

Sift a coat of 2030 Medium Fusing Clear over the entire surface and fire. This technique changes the colors and adds interest and depth to the surface.

If using beryl green or another transparent color that contains a lot of oxides, it can be exciting to play the flame over the top after the enamel reaches the orange-peel stage when fired from underneath. Bring the flame close and then take it away, watching the color develop.

Oxides rise to the surface, creating a beautiful sheen.

Anat's
gallery

I used many of the enameling techniques you've learned in this book to create the pieces on these four pages. The following two pages showcase the work of some of my talented students. I hope you are inspired by our designs.

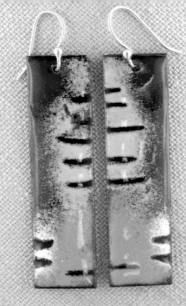

Student
gallery

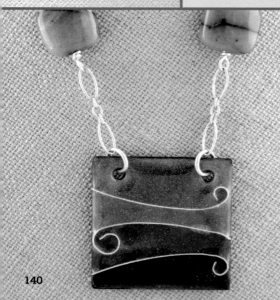

Facing page (clockwise from top left): Joanna Konarzewski, Rhoda Cataleta, Natalie Knott, Lynn Ackerson, Valery Tkachenko.

This page (clockwise from top right): Valery Tkachenko, Lynn Ackerson, Valery Tkachenko, Joanna Konarzewski, Susan DeBock, Paul Kmetko.

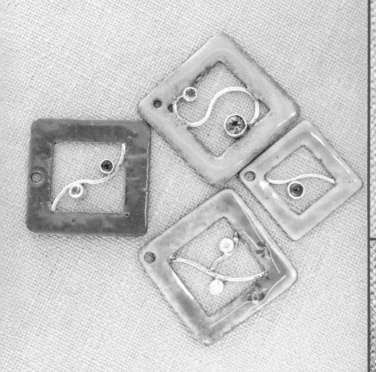

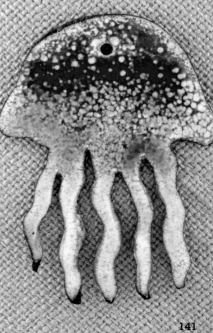

resources

beaducation.com
Enamel kits, kiln bricks

enameling.com
Tools, supplies, lead-free enamels

enamelworksupply.com
Small containers, tools, leaded enamels

halsteadbead.com
Fine-silver disks, copper

silverajewelry.com
Metalsmithing tools, copper shapes, tools, supplies

thompsonenamel.com
Tools and supplies

Check out your local bead shop for chain and findings to make your enameled treasures wearable, tools, and possibly even enameling supplies. Two of my favorites in California's Bay area, where I live and work, are Leslie Ceramics and Baubles and Beads.

acknowledgments

Thank you to Emily Miller for introducing me to torch-fired enameling years ago. You sparked my imagination.

My sincerest thanks to everyone at Kalmbach Books for the opportunity to write this book, especially my editor, Mary Wohlgemuth, who was always there with encouragement and respect for my dreams for this project. I can't thank the team enough for their attention to detail, fabulous layout, and marketing know-how.

Many thanks to Natalie Knott, for being a wonderful friend and project guinea pig, reading drafts and lending her support with her time and energy.

Maggie Miglio, thank you for your great sense of humor and friendship, especially when I was frustrated. Your cool shoes (a different pair every day) kept my spirits up amidst the chaos of writing.

My dear friend Julie Scheinman, I so appreciate your unflagging support and your willingness to take me on much-needed escapes when I needed them most.

My mentor, teacher, and dear friend, Gabrielle Castonguay, who is such an amazing enamel artist—you boosted my confidence! Thank you for reading my final draft and for your feedback. Your praise and respect for my work honors and thrills me.

Thanks to Lisa Kaufman for your support and a great photo of me.

Thank you to Lynn Ackerson, Rhoda Cataleta, Susan DeBock, Paul Kmetko, Natalie Knott, Joanna Konarzewski, and Valery Tkachenko for sharing your work in this book.

Loving thanks to my sweet dogs, Bela and Django, who were always there for a cuddle break.

And, of course, heartfelt thanks to my dear, wonderful husband and partner, Joe. Your faith in my abilities as an artist and writer is unwavering. I could not have done this without all of your loving support.

about the author

LISA KAUFMAN PHOTO

ANAT SILVERA has loved jewelry since she was a little girl growing up in Los Angeles. Before and after college she studied with artists and craftsmen, apprenticing as a metalsmith and learning how to create fine beadwork. Anat has exhibited and sold her work all over the U.S., including in an exhibit as a featured artist at the Oakland Museum of Art Collectors Gallery. Anat is a member of the Northern California Enamel Guild and the Enamelist Society.

Anat combines her love of enamel color and metal in the daily pursuit of jewelry making and discovers new ways to help her students explore their creativity. She teaches an array of jewelry-making skills at Silvera Jewelry School in Berkeley, Calif. (silverajewelryschool.com), which she runs with her husband, Joe Silvera. She also teaches at Baubles and Beads, Alaska Bead Company, and the Bead&Button Show.

index

Professional soldering techniques
for the home jewelry maker

Soldering Made Simple is like taking a master class by a master craftsman!

Joe Silvera teaches you how to use a handheld butane torch to solder nearly any small-scale jewelry project with success. You'll start with a review of the basics and then put your skills to use making 12 charming projects.

Soldering Made Simple
Easy techniques for the kitchen-table jeweler

JOE SILVERA

64063 • $21.95

15074 • $19.95

Joe's companion DVD demonstrates his techniques in action. Watch as he explains everything you'll need to get started, and then creates a beautiful soldered pendant and necklace. A PDF with step-by-step instructions is also included!